K-DRAMA

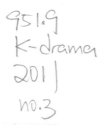

KOREAN CULTURE NO.3

K-Drama: A New TV Genre with Global Appeal

Copyright © 2011
by Korean Culture and Information Service

First Published in 2011 by
Korean Culture and Information Service
Ministry of Culture, Sports and Tourism

Phone: 82-2-398-1914~20
Fax: 82-2-398-1882
Website: www.kocis.go.kr

ISBN: 978-89-7375-167-9 04600
ISBN: 978-89-7375-163-1 (set)

Printed in the Republic of Korea

For further information about Korea, please visit:
www.korea.net

K-DRAMA

A New TV Genre with Global Appeal

Contents

"South Korea's soppy soaps win hearts across Asia.
Hallyu is not just spreading culture out from Korea,
it is also drawing people in."

Anna Fifield, *The Financial Times*, December 14, 2004

"In China, South Korean dramas are sold, and pirated,
everywhere, and the young adopt the clothing and hairstyles
made cool by South Korean stars. South Korea, historically
more worried about fending off cultural domination by China
and Japan than spreading its own culture abroad, is emerging
as the pop culture leader of Asia."

Norimitsu Onishi, *The New York Times*, June 29, 2005

"*Forget* Desperate Housewives *or* Survivor. *In Asia,* The
Jewel in the Palace *and* Winter Sonata *are the must-see
television shows. South Korea is cashing in on a marketing
push that has made its soap operas and pop stars wildly
popular across Asia.* "

Louisa Lim, National Public Radio (U.S.A), March 26, 2006

"The popular K-Dramas I've seen, even the most recent
ones, feel like throwbacks to a less cynical time. ...
They're really charming, funny shows."

Stephan Lee, *Entertainment Weekly,* February 2, 2011

PROLOGUE

Until the 1980s, Korean television networks were like a theater for staging foreign shows. American productions drew the attention of Korean audiences, while Japanese productions captured the hearts of animation fans.

Back then, the importation of Japanese popular culture was officially banned, but its huge influence on Korean television productions was difficult to conceal. In particular, increasing overseas travel and the development of video and digital mass media allowed for an influx of Japanese culture into domestic industries, while the widespread viewership enjoyed by cable networks broke down boundaries between the two nations. Japanese television programs proved a useful source of important ideas for the planning and production of Korean television shows.

But as the Korean government began to lift its ban on the distribution and sale of Japanese popular culture in 1998, a wide array of Japanese cultural products were imported and reworked into Korean versions to suit local tastes.

In addition to this new openness to Japanese popular culture, the period also saw more and more cooperation and hybrid efforts within the cultural industries of the two nations, each enriching the other's cultural products and allowing for the development of a unique Korean culture in the

production and development process.

Meanwhile, although American television series such as *CSI*, *Grey's Anatomy*, *Prison Break*, and *Friends* have met with an enthusiastic response from Korean viewers in recent years, the connection between Korean audiences and American television shows has a history that goes back even further. For many Koreans in their 40s and 50s who grew up watching old American shows like *The Six Million Dollar Man*, *The A-Team*, and *MacGyver* on prime time in the 1980s, American television shows might evoke nostalgic memories, as there was little else in the way of major entertainment. The heroic storylines and spectacular action of the American television series were difficult to find in their Korean counterparts. They mesmerized Korean audiences and exerted an influence on their later emotional development.

For such viewers, the meteoric rise of Korean television series (commonly called "dramas") as a globally

A younger devotee at a March 2007 fan meeting for Hallyu star Song Seung-hun

Japanese fans welcome Bae Yong-joon at Haneda International Airport in April 2011.

appreciated form of entertainment seems like the perfect ending to the unlikeliest of scripts.

It could be said, then, that the line between fantasy and reality has never been thinner. After winning over Asian viewers in recent years, Korean soap operas now seem to be on the verge of a worldwide breakthrough, enjoying a rapidly widening fan base that includes more and more Americans and Europeans. This has been coupled with an unprecedented cultural influence that even the shows' delighted creators have yet to fully understand or embrace.

While Korean television companies might need more time for the growing prominence of their products to sink in, it is also critical that they avoid buying into their own hype and falling victim to unrealistic expectations. As Korean dramas extend their reach to farther-flung audiences, it remains to be seen whether they are destined to be part of an even grander achievement or fizzle out as one-hit wonders. It would be meaningful, then, to take a closer look at what has been driving the popularity of Korean dramas, how they have benefited from advancements in Internet and mobile technologies, and whether those factors will add up to staying power.

Chapter One

K-DRAMA
AND HALLYU

K-Drama: The Beginning of Hallyu

"Hallyu," which literally means "Korean wave," is a term that was first coined in China by Beijing journalists in the mid-1990s to describe the fast-growing popularity of Korean entertainment and culture in that country. Referring to an appreciation for Korean cultural exports, it first entered common parlance in 2003 when *Winter Sonata* (*Gyeoul Yeonga*), a Korean television series starring the now-iconic Bae Yong-joon, created a massive sensation with its airing on Japanese television. It should also be noted that Hallyu was something of an overstatement in terms of what was actually happening back then. Despite the striking image of millions of middle-aged Japanese women going ga-ga over "Yonsama" (as Bae is called by his legion of Japanese fans), the acceptance of Korean dramas was still limited to a few shows.

Fast forward to 2011, and what was once considered a strictly Asian phenomenon appears poised to spread through the entire world. Many of the dramas made in past years by Korea's "big three" national channels—KBS, MBC, and SBS—are now finding their way to practically every corner of the globe, from Japan and China to North America, Europe, the Middle East, and Africa. The bigger Korean television stars are coming under the pan-Asian spotlight, while the filming locations of their hit dramas have become major tourist destinations in Korea for pilgrimages by an endless string of foreign fans.

China: Where Hallyu Began

The burgeoning love of Korean popular culture was first triggered by Korean television series that aired in China in the late 1990s. One of these

Feature page on sohu.com, a Chinese portal site that selects the top Korean drama stars by Internet voting

was *What Is Love?* (starring veteran actors Lee Sun-jae and Kim Hye-ja), which was broadcast in June 1997 on China Central Television (CCTV). With a story about two different families—a traditional conservative Korean family and a westernized, open-minded family—who end up in conflict over the marriage of their children, the drama was enormously

(Top) *What is Love*
(Bottom) *A Wish Upon a Star*

popular with the Chinese audience for its portrayal of Confucian values, emphasizing the importance of family tradition while including humorous touches. As the soap opera's audience share reached 15 percent, the second highest ever for an imported program in China, it sparked a general interest in Korean dramas. The enthusiastic response was immediately reciprocated with *Star in My Heart*, a series starring Choi Jin-sil and Ahn Jae-wook that was first broadcast on Phoenix TV on Hong Kong before heading to the mainland.

A series of successes by Korean dramas paved the way for many Korean singers to debut in China, Hong Kong, and Taiwan. The success of Korean dramas in China was significant in that the "Hallyu" idea was prompted by the Korean drama boom and would lead to an infatuation with Korean popular culture among the Chinese public, one that was widely discussed by Beijing journalists after the coining of the term "Hallyu" in 1999.

The popularity of Korean cultural products in China has only grown since then and continues to influence the country's trends and styles in television shows, movies, music, and video games. And with Hallyu fever infecting neighboring nations like Taiwan, Vietnam, Thailand, and Mongolia as well, Korean content creators have set their sights on the United States and Europe. The early returns are promising.

Although K-pop has been getting much media coverage lately, Korean television products continue to lead the upward trend. While it's debatable how much room Korean dramas have left for growth or whether their level of popularity is sustainable, it's also worth mentioning that they have already lasted longer in the international limelight than most originally imagined.

So what's behind the appeal, popularity, and following of Korean dramas? Perhaps there are several ways to approach the question, but any evaluation will have to start with *Winter Sonata*, a breakthrough moment that continues to serve as a blueprint.

Winter Sonata Touches Off Korean Drama Craze in Japan

Although Korean music and movies had been gaining a Japanese following since the late 1990s, the popularity of *Winter Sonata*, a 20-part KBS series that first aired back home in 2002 before reaching Japanese viewers through NHK's satellite channel the following year, was impressive in its intensity and suddenness.

It could be argued that *Winter Sonata* adhered to a basic formula for television success: beautiful people (in this case, Bae Yong-joon and female counterpart Choi Ji-woo), beautiful scenery (snow-covered Nami Island), and a syrup-drenched plot built on love, death, and helpless romantic longing, all played out against a soundtrack of melancholy music.

Everything clicked right away, and *Winter Sonata* morphed into a national sensation in Japan that greatly outstripped the popularity the drama had garnered from its original broadcasts in Korea. By the final episode, NHK was getting an audience share of over 20 percent, a staggering figure in a country where even prime time shows rarely reach a 10 percent rating. By the end of 2004, it was estimated that nearly 70 percent of Japanese viewers had watched at least one episode.

This was an unprecedented response, given that *Winter Sonata* aired at 11 p.m. and the eyes of the Japanese audience were fixed on broadcasts of the 2004 Olympic Games in Athens. In fact, the average audience share was particularly astonishing in light of the fact that *Shinsengumi*, a prime time Japanese epic drama series that had been airing on NHK since January 11, 2004, had achieved only a 17.7 percent rating.

Actor Bae Yong-joon and actress Choi Ji-woo of *Winter Sonata*.

Bae Yong-joon and Choi Ji-woo—or Ji-woo Hime (Princess Ji-woo), as she was affectionately known in Japan—found themselves on the receiving end of the enthusiastic greetings normally reserved for A-list Hollywood celebrities. Their newfound popularity was even mentioned by Japanese Prime Minister Junichiro Koizumi, who joked that "Yonsama is more popular than me" in a symposium on "The Future of Asia" held in Tokyo in 2004, and pled to be called "Jun-sama" during one election speech.

Winter Sonata's influence in Japan was felt far beyond the realm of popular culture. It reached into society, business, and even the dusty halls of academia. Korean language schools in Japan enjoyed a bonanza thanks to a sudden increase in people wishing to learn the language, while Korean locations used in the drama benefited from a rush of Japanese tourism. Sales soared for Korean popular culture-related products such as books, magazines, DVDs, and accessories, while Hallyu-themed websites and blogs began popping up like mushrooms.

The *Winter Sonata* boom was quickly and dramatically reshaping the way the Japanese saw and understood Korea's culture and people, evoking both awe and apprehension from Japanese media, which seemed unsure what to make of it all.

Jewel in the Palace Elevates Hallyu to New Levels beyond Asia

While it would be difficult to overstate the influence of *Winter Sonata*, it is indisputable that *Jewel in the Palace* (*Daejanggeum*), which first aired on MBC in 2003, was just as pivotal, if not more so, in elevating Hallyu to new levels.

In stylistic terms, the two dramas couldn't be more different. *Winter Sonata* shares the DNA of classic tearjerkers like Arthur Hiller's *Love Story* and Shunji Iwai's *Love Letter*, one of the first Japanese films shown in Korea after the country began lifting its import ban on Japanese cultural goods in 1998. In contrast, *Jewel in the Palace*, starring popular actress Lee Young-ae, is a period drama set during the reign of King Jungjong (1506-1544) of the Joseon Dynasty (1392-1910). It tells the tale of an orphaned kitchen cook who goes on to become the king's first female physician.

Not in their wildest dreams could *Jewel in the Palace*'s creators have imagined reaching an audience much wider than its domestic viewership. After all, the drama's Korean historical and cultural backdrop would seem to restrict its appeal. But this didn't keep *Jewel in the Palace* from becoming Korea's first true worldwide television hit.

Although *Winter Sonata* had essentially been a two-nation obsession, *Jewel in the Palace* was broadcast in many more countries. The buzz surrounding the show came from nearly every corner of the planet. Whereas *Winter Sonata* had been exported to 20 countries, *Jewel in the Palace* was sold to 87 countries as of May 2011—proof of its worldwide popularity.

Major Countries Airing *Jewel in the Palace* (year)

Uzbekistan (2007)
Hungary (2008)
Afghanistan (2007)
Ukraine (2009)
Japan (2006)
Kazakhstan (2006)
Romania (2009)
Turkey (2009)
Israel (2007)
Taiwan (2004)
Egypt (2006)
China (2005)
Iran (2006)
Hong Kong (2005)
Algeria (2008)
Philippines (2005)
Ghana (2008)
India (2007)
Vietnam (2004)
Nigeria (2008)
Kenya (2009)
Thailand (2005)
Tanzania (2007)
Ethiopia (2009)
Malaysia (2005)
Zimbabwe (2007)
Australia (2005)
Singapore (2006)
Zambia (2008)
Indonesia (2006)

Academic Studies on Hallyu

The international social and cultural changes and reshaping of historical currents that *Winter Sonata* brought to Japan and Korea have become a major topic for academic research.

Arvind Singhal, a professor of communication studies at Ohio University, and Toru Hanaki, a professor of communication studies at the Faculty of Foreign Studies of Nazan University, collaborated with other researchers on a paper titled "Hanryu Sweeps East Asia: How *Winter Sonata* is Gripping Japan," which was printed between 2005 and 2007 in the world-renowned communication journal *The International Communication Gazette*.

According to the research, *Winter Sonata* is a rare example of the popularity of a television drama playing a key role in a different cultural zone.

In the early 20th century, the Japanese imperialist occupation left deep emotional scars on Korea and other Asian countries. Members of the country's largest ethnic minority—ethnic Koreans who were forcibly moved to Japan during the war—were subjected to discrimination as second-class citizens due to economic difficulties and remained an invisible presence in mainstream Japanese society.

For Japanese people who remember the years of colonial rule (1910-45) and the Korean War (1950-53), Korea was a close but distant country. However, the Hallyu phenomenon sparked by *Winter Sonata* greatly changed the Japanese people's perceptions of Koreans.

In response to a question on the ways in which *Winter Sonata* and the accompanying Hallyu phenomenon changed Japanese women's perceptions of Zainichi Koreans, one company employee in her 50s said, "Although South Korea is a neighboring country, I did not try to know the country, and I even looked down on it. Now I want to know South Korea and try to know South Korea. A country that is geographically close but psychologically far became a country that is both geographically and psychologically close."

Singhal also collaborated with Han Min-wha on a research paper titled "Forced

Invisibility to Negotiating Visibility: *Winter Sonata*, The Hanryu Phenomenon and Zainichi Koreans in Japan." In this study, the team attempted an in-depth look into the social effects *Winter Sonata* and other Korean cultural exports were having in Japan by helping Korean residents in Japan improve their social standing and turning them from "invisible" to "visible" presences in Japanese society.

The Korean cultural boom triggered dramatic changes in Japanese attitudes, which also helped ethnic Koreans to gain recognition for their unique identity and social position in Japan.

The researchers talked about further changes in perceptions: "*Winter Sonata*'s popularity in Japan and the *hanryu* phenomenon have increased trade between the two countries and promoted people-exchanges. *Winter Sonata* fuelled the interest of Japanese citizens to learn more about South Korea. Many Japanese enrolled in Korean language courses, and thousands traveled to South Korea to sites where *Winter Sonata* was filmed."

(Top) Akie, the wife of former Japanese Prime Minister Shinzo Abe, is known to be a big Hallyu fan. (Middle) "Hanryu Sweeps East Asia," a dissertation on *Winter Sonata*. (Bottom) Shim Jong-il, a third–generation Korean in Japan, was able to perform in Korean in a traditional Japanese comedy thanks to the Hallyu fever.

The list of countries hit by the frenzy for *Jewel in the Palace* reads like a United Nations roll call. The drama was a massive hit in nearly all of Asia's sizable television markets, from Japan, China, Hong Kong, Taiwan, and India to Thailand, Malaysia, Indonesia, the Philippines, Vietnam, Singapore, and Brunei.

And it wasn't a phenomenon limited to the Asia-Pacific, either. *Jewel in the Palace* found a significant following among viewers in North America and Europe, as well as in countries like Russia, Turkey, Israel, Saudi Arabia, and Iran. Eventually, the show was broadcast in more than 87 countries worldwide. Furthermore, it seemed that the drama's 16th century Korean setting was adding to its global appeal instead of hurting it.

The story of a humble but dedicated woman overcoming all odds and neo-Confucianist values to become a royal physician touched the hearts of viewers from diverse cultures, many of them sharing the pre-modern experience of oppression against women and their social roles. And the drama's dazzling depictions of traditional architecture, music, attire, food, and medicine gave foreign fans a distinctive taste of Korea's culture and heritage.

K-Drama Reaches into Asia and Beyond

The stunning success of *Jewel in the Palace* marked a watershed moment in the globalization of Korean dramas, which saw their target audience expand from Asians to viewers in the Western world as well as in the Middle East and Africa. Today, there is high demand for Korean soap operas even in countries where Korean television networks haven't been able to ink broadcasting deals.

Asia

One particular example is Nepal, where fans have been enthusiastically consuming Korean dramas through the Internet and DVDs imported from China, India, and Thailand. As in Japan, the Korean drama frenzy in Nepal was triggered by *Winter Sonata* and has since extended to the series *Boys Over Flowers*, *Coffee Prince*, and *You Are Beautiful*. Young Nepalese women appear to be the country's most spirited followers of Korean dramas, thanks to male stars like Bae Yong-joon and scripts that make them look even better. In the Nepalese capital of Kathmandu, an increasing number of youngsters have been spotted emulating Korean fashion trends. As was the case in Japan, Korean language courses are experiencing a boom there.

Republica, a vernacular newspaper based in Kathmandu, published an article titled "Ubiquitous Korean Wave" in its edition of March 7, 2010. The piece observed the way that the market for Korean products was growing

You Are Beautiful was a hit that aired in over 17 countries.

by the day, encompassing everything from dramas and movies to food and clothes. "The urban youth today prefer everything Korean," it read.

Korean dramas are just as hot in the Philippines, where they are affectionately called "Koreanovelas." The term was created by GMA Network, a major commercial television and radio station in the Philippines, in response to the growing popularity of Korean dramas, following in the footsteps of the success of Mexican telenovelas and Taiwanese dramas. The country's major broadcasters, including GMA Network and ABS-CBN, are competing to import more and more Korean dramas, which are often slotted during prime time hours and relied upon to carry the networks' audience shares. Most of the Korean dramas broadcast locally are dubbed into Filipino. Many Filipino viewers say they were attracted to Korean dramas because they are less provocative and violent than local dramas or other imported shows. This perhaps explains the high ratings for *Boys Over Flowers*, the quintessential "pretty boy" drama.

Among the newest markets for Korean dramas are Central Asia and former Soviet republics in the Commonwealth of Independent States (CIS). Since 2003 the state-run broadcaster in Uzbekistan has aired a slew of Korean dramas, including *Winter Sonata*, *Jewel in the Palace*, *Damo*, and *Jumong*. Korean historical dramas such as *Jumong*, *Hong Gil-dong*, *Yi San*, and *Heo Jun* struck a chord with television audiences in Kazakhstan as well, although younger viewers seemed to prefer romantic dramas such as *Autumn in My Heart*, *First Love*, and *All In*.

Korean dramas are also big in Vietnam. In a 2008 survey by the Vietnamese Internet news site VnExpress, *Jewel in the Palace* was picked as the country's favorite Korean television import, garnering nearly 39 percent of the votes. Historical dramas, mostly Chinese ones, have always been a big part of Vietnamese television entertainment, and this appears to have laid the foundation for the success of Korean period pieces like *Jewel in the Palace*, *Jumong*, and *The Legend*. The younger Vietnamese audience appears to be gravitating toward big-name Hallyu stars like Song Hye-kyo and Rain, who were paired in the romantic drama *Full House*. Korean singer and actress Yun Eun-hye emerged as a popular celebrity in Vietnam due to the popularity of *The Palace*, as did fellow female star Lee Da-hae after the airing of *My Girl*.

The Korean drama frenzy in Thailand is summed up in comments made by former Prime Minister Abhisit Vejjajiva, in a 2009 interview with the local media that he followed the works of Korea's biggest television stars

Director and stars of *Coffee Prince* at a production presentation

The romantic drama *Full House*

because his daughter was a Hallyu fan. He said he had a stack of DVDs of Korean dramas that he popped in every once in a while, and that he frequently took his family out to dine in Korean restaurants in Bangkok.

The Korean drama frenzy in Thailand actually started earlier than in most Asian countries, but it appeared to wane a bit in the mid-2000s after shows like *Sangdo* and *Iutjib Yeoja* met with only a lukewarm reception. But the airing of *My Girl* in 2007 would mark the start of a ferocious rebound. The popularity of Korean dramas went on to hit a new peak in the years following the broadcasts of *Coffee Prince*, a romantic drama carried by Yun Eun-hye and male counterpart Gong Yoo, and *The Legend*, which starred Bae Yong-joon of *Winter Sonata* fame.

Indonesia has been brimming with Hallyu culture ever since Korea was jointly picked to host the 2002 World Cup with Japan, which helped lift the image of the country and its culture. The popularity of Korean culture was boosted by *Autumn in My Heart*, which aired on Indosiar television from July to August 2002 and gained an 11 percent audience share during its run. Then *Winter Sonata* arrived, and the Hallyu boom in Indonesia shifted into top gear. More than 50 Korean dramas have been shown on Indonesian television since then, and consumers have been racking up purchases of DVDs, CDs, and other merchandise. Indosiar continues to be the country's leading source of Korean dramas, which are usually placed in the coveted 4 to 9 p.m. time slot. The biggest hit has been *Full House*, which posted a staggering viewership rate of nearly 40 percent when it aired in 2005.

Hallyu appears to be rattling the multicultural hotpot that is Malaysia as well. Most DVD stores in major Malaysian cities have separate sections for Korean dramas. The most popular titles for DVD renters include *Winter Sonata*, *Heo Jun*, and *Full House*, all of which generated significant buzz after airing on local television networks. *Jewel in the Palace*, which has been considered the favorite Korean drama among Malaysians, was dubbed into several languages, including Mandarin, Cantonese, and Malay, and has already been broadcast an unprecedented three times. The drama's popularity sparked a new demand for Korean food, as evidenced by the slew of restaurants named Daejanggeum that have appeared in the years since.

Middle East

While the Korean drama frenzy in Asian countries was understandable given the cultural affinity, its popularity in other regions like the Middle East was a more surprising development. In its 2006 debut on Iranian national television, *Jewel in the Palace* achieved a 57 percent audience share, which remains as an extremely difficult standard to match. Based on a survey conducted by IRIB (Islamic Republic of Iran Broadcasting), this series was ranked as the most popular drama on the network from March to April 2007, with 92 percent satisfaction rate.

The show's immense popularity in Iran led to a variety of theories to explain the phenomenon. Some pointed out that *Jewel in the Palace* reminded Iranians of *Oshin*, a popular Japanese drama that had aired in the country two decades earlier. Others wondered whether viewers were

The period drama *Jumong* tells the story of the king who established Goguryeo, the first modern nation on the Korean Peninsula.

(Left) *Jewel in the Palace* also touched off a Korean cuisine boom.
(Right) Iranian magazine cover featuring Lee Young-ae

sympathizing with lead character Janggeum (Lee Young-ae), a young palace girl from a lower-class background who successfully works her way up to become the personal physician of the king. The storyline seemed to have a universal appeal that transcended Korea's own cultural emphasis on maintaining social status, according to Ulara Nakagawa, a writer for the magazine *The Diplomat*.

The cultural impact of *Jewel in the Palace* in Iran was significant. Tens of thousands of websites and blogs were devoted to the show, and the number of Iranian learners of Korean skyrocketed. Iranians living in Korea even created a blog (iraniankorea.blogfa.com) to teach their countrymen how to speak and write in Korean.

The show's huge success also paved the way for other period dramas like *Jumong*, which enjoyed high ratings in Iran. The Korean actors appearing in the dramas earned top dollar from Iranian advertisers. In particular, *Jumong*, which aired on IRIB in 2008, received an astonishing 85 percent viewership rate.

Jewel in the Palace garnered a positive response from viewers in Turkey, Jordan, Egypt, Israel, and Nigeria as well.

North America

Of course, it would be awkward for Korean television companies to speechify about globalization without making noise in the US, the undisputed television capital of the world. And it seems they are beginning to do just that.

The television relationship between Korea and the US has always been lopsided. For decades, Korean viewers have continued to gravitate toward popular American shows like *CSI*, *Grey's Anatomy*, and *Prison Break*, while the existence of Korean television entertainment has remained unknown to American viewers.

But it appears that a number of Korean dramas are starting to find their way into the hearts of American viewers, many of whom stay up until

The *Coffee Prince* page on Hulu, the US's top video service. The show earned a high rating of four-and-a-half stars.

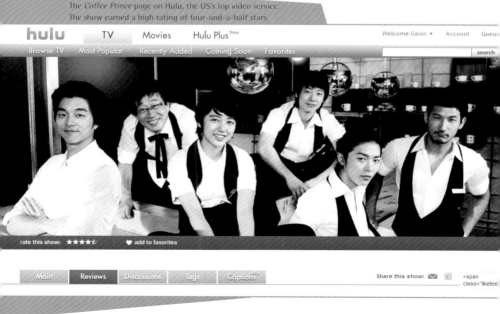

the wee hours with bloodshot eyes watching episodes of their favorite shows on video websites like Hulu. One of the Korean dramas successfully drawing an American audience has been *Coffee Prince*, while SBS's recent hit *Secret Garden*, a romantic comedy starring Hyun Bin and female counterpart Ha Ji-won, has been gathering significant online traffic as well. *Coffee Prince* was among a handful of Korean dramas that ranked among the 200 most-watched shows on Hulu

Secret Garden

as of February 2011. In addition to Hulu, Drama Fever and Drama Crazy are popular Internet destinations for American fans of Korean dramas.

The increasing popularity of Korean dramas was even depicted in the romantic fantasy movie *Beastly*, released earlier this year. In the film, which stars Vanessa Hudgens and Alex Pettyfer, the two main characters grow closer by sharing their affection for a Korean soap opera, which was specially produced for the film.

According to a 2008 report from the Korea Foundation for International Culture Exchange (KOFICE) on the patterns of media acceptance by American audiences, more active approaches to consumption using personal computers and mobile gadgets, rather than passive reliance on living room's flat screens, have significantly affected the decision-making process of audiences, which has had a positive effect on the viewing of Korean dramas in the United States. This marks a quantum leap from

The **world** **is** **watching**
K-Drama

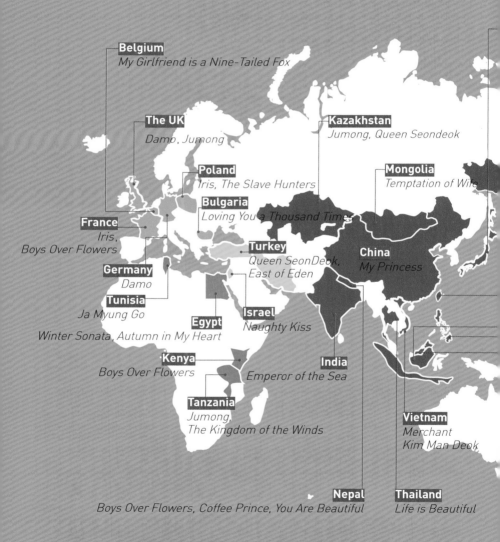

Belgium
My Girlfriend is a Nine-Tailed Fox

The UK
Damo, Jumong

Kazakhstan
Jumong, Queen Seondeok

Poland
Iris, The Slave Hunters

Mongolia
Temptation of Wife

Bulgaria
Loving You a Thousand Times

France
Iris,
Boys Over Flowers

Turkey
Queen SeonDeok,
East of Eden

China
My Princess

Germany
Damo

Tunisia
Ja Myung Go
Winter Sonata, Autumn in My Heart

Egypt

Israel
Naughty Kiss

Kenya
Boys Over Flowers

India
Emperor of the Sea

Tanzania
Jumong,
The Kingdom of the Winds

Vietnam
Merchant
Kim Man Deok

Nepal
Boys Over Flowers, Coffee Prince, You Are Beautiful

Thailand
Life is Beautiful

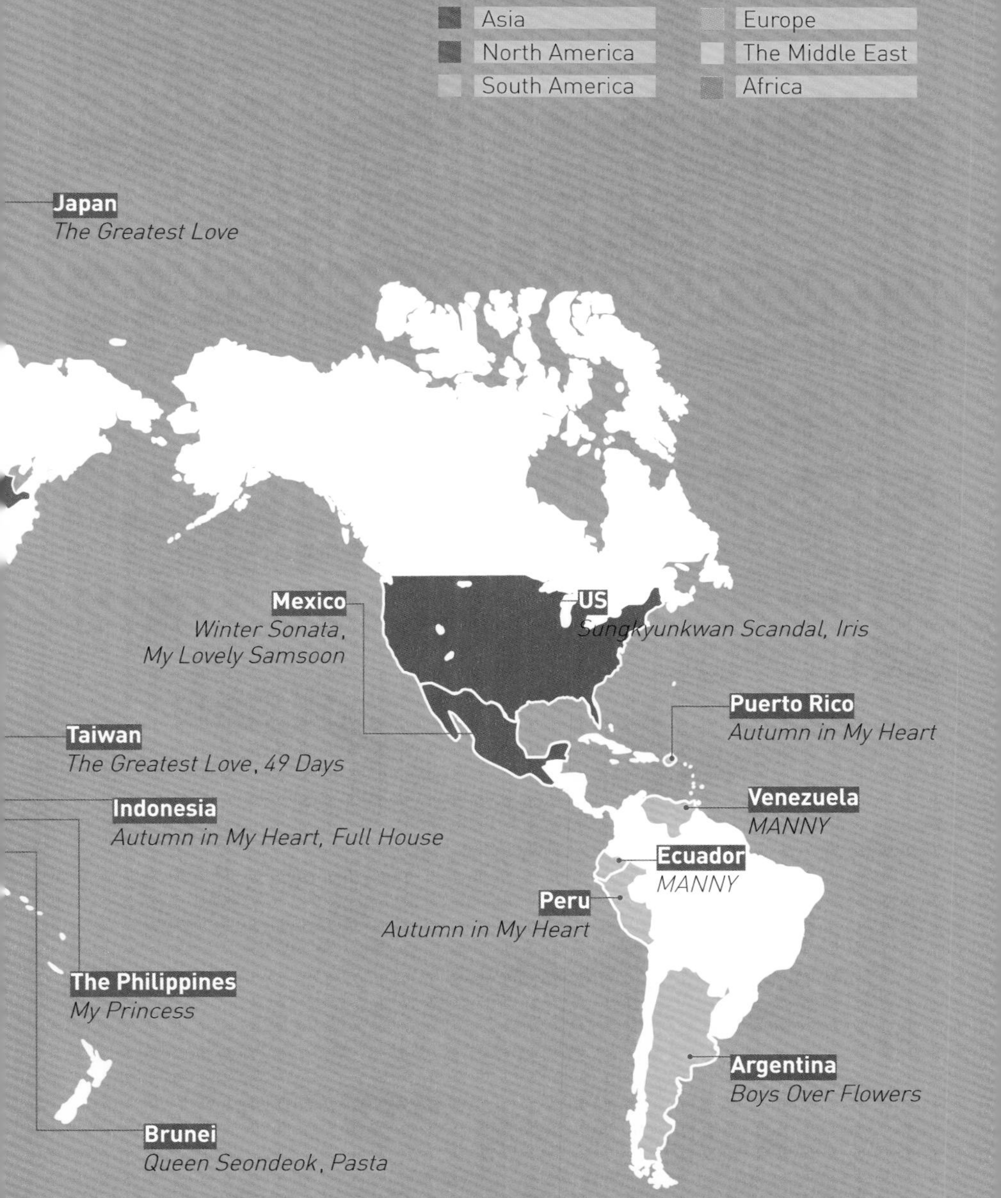

Asia
North America
South America
Europe
The Middle East
Africa

Japan
The Greatest Love

Mexico
Winter Sonata,
My Lovely Samsoon

US
Sungkyunkwan Scandal, Iris

Puerto Rico
Autumn in My Heart

Taiwan
The Greatest Love, 49 Days

Indonesia
Autumn in My Heart, Full House

Venezuela
MANNY

Ecuador
MANNY

Peru
Autumn in My Heart

The Philippines
My Princess

Argentina
Boys Over Flowers

Brunei
Queen Seondeok, Pasta

the days when the shows were only available through Asian video rental stores.

Korean language channels in the US that have been airing Korean dramas with English dubbing are now enjoying a sudden surge in viewership, and the dramas are reaching other channels as well. Numerous American websites, including the Korean Drama Group, are now devoted to Korean soap operas. Predictably, Daejanggeum has become a popular name for Asian restaurants in US cities.

South America

In Brazil, the consumption of Korean dramas was first driven by Korean expatriates and immigrants. But the shows are now reaching a much wider audience, including a very supportive Japanese community. Korean television shows, movies, and music videos with Japanese dubbing or subtitles have become important products in Brazil's video and DVD rental shops due to the country's large Japanese population.

In Mexico, *Winter Sonata*, *My Lovely Samsoon*, *All About Eve*, *Autumn in My Heart*, *Star in My Heart*, and *Four Sisters* aired on the country's public network Mexiquense, with *My Lovely Samsoon* emerging as a hit. Viewership of Korean dramas has been picking up in nearby countries like Costa Rica, Venezuela, Peru, and Puerto Rico as well. Peruvian viewers were particularly fond of *Autumn in My Heart*, which aired on TV Peru for the first time in 2007 and re-aired on the network recently. The network also aired *Jewel in the Palace* between late 2008 and 2009.

Europe and Africa

The fastest-growing new markets for Korean dramas in the first half of 2011 were Europe and South and Central America, according to an August 2011 report by the Korea Creative Content Agency (KOCCA).

KBS recently inked a deal with the French media company DoubleV over local broadcasting rights for its action-adventure series *Iris*, while its teen romance *Boys Over Flowers* has been exported to France, Mexico, Peru, Argentina, and Kenya. MBC's romantic drama *Naughty Kiss* will now be reaching Israeli viewers, and the broadcaster continues to find demand for *Jewel in the Palace*, which is now to be shown in Romania.

Hallyu fans in Bulgaria. In February 2011, the drama *Loving You a Thousand Times* was shown on Bulgarian television.

Korean Dramas in the Eyes of International Fan Clubs

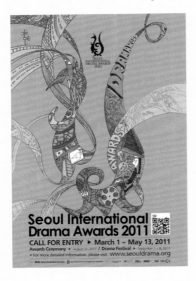

The sixth Seoul International Drama Awards (SDA) were held at KBS Hall in Yeouido on August 31, 2011, with Hallyu stars and fans from across the globe in attendance. A total of 204 dramas from 37 countries were submitted with 39 of them making it to the finals. Since its inception in 2006, the drama festival has attracted Hallyu supporters from around the World. The 2011 event invited overseas Korean drama fan communities from France, Romania, Peru, Chile, and Mexico.

In a report on August 30, 2011, *The Korea Times* noted the festival visit by heads of international fan clubs. Maxime Paquet, president of the France-based organization Korean Connection, said Korean dramas were interesting because they introduced the essence of Korean culture through love, happiness, and sadness. Paquet was optimistic about the future of the Korean Wave, saying, "I think the support of the Korean government and companies will be key in spreading Korean culture all over the world."

Daniela Predut of the Romanian Korean Intercultural Association (RKIA) said Korean epic dramas started airing in Romania in 2009 and that the RKIA was established to promote Korean culture, particularly dramas. *Jumong* was seen by some 800,000 viewers during its early 2011 broadcast in Romania.

"We now have about 30,000 members and are trying to promote other parts of Korean culture such as history and food as well," Predut said. "Last week, the first K-pop music program was launched in Romania. Now, we can listen to K-pop every day on television."

The Korea Herald also had a story on August 29 about Miluska Cabrera from Peru, who said that there were some 40 Hallyu fan clubs in her country. KBS's *Boys Over Flowers* was one the most popular shows, with its lead actors Lee Min-ho and Kim Hyun-joong. "All Peruvians have seen at least one Korean drama," Cabrera said. She also said the popularity of Korean dramas was due to their being a departure from typical telenovelas.

The heads of overseas Hallyu fan clubs at the 2011 Seoul International Drama Awards: (left to right) Daniela Predut from Romania, Maxime Paquet from France, and Miluska Cabrera from Peru.

Internet is blurring the boundaries of time, geography

The international popularity of Korean dramas has shifted into a higher gear since the emergence of video streaming websites and social networking during the 2000s.

The Internet continues to change the way people read, think, and exchange ideas, a shakeup that has been jolted by such social media as blogs, Facebook, and Twitter. This dramatic reshaping shows the new ways that cultural products are consumed, shared, and remembered. Combine this with the rapid growth of online video services like YouTube, Hulu, and Netflix, and it appears that the consumption of traditional television is turning into a supercharged social experience that is blurring the boundaries of time, geography, and language.

On June 21, 2011, MBC, the country's second-ranked national television network, unveiled a special YouTube-only edition of *Naughty Kiss*, a romantic comedy with a teen-friendly cast led by pop heartthrob Kim Hyun-joong. The episodes, along with related clips including cast interviews and a documentary on how the drama was made, have together drawn more than 20 million hits, and fans have been enthusiastic enough to post subtitles in English, Chinese, Japanese, and Spanish.

Hulu Establishes a New Category for Korean Dramas

Currently, Hulu lists 25 different television genres to serve the preferences of its wide variety of viewers. Included in the mix is the category of "Korean Drama," one of only a few categories based on national origin or language. This suggests that the dramas are becoming addictive for American viewers as well.

Among the self-professed K-Drama addicts is Stephan Lee, a writer for American magazine *Entertainment Weekly*, who said he became "hooked" after watching the KBS show *Boys Over*

Hulu page for *Boys Over Flowers*

Flowers on Hulu.

"I watched all 25 episodes of the series and had serious withdrawal after it ended," Lee wrote on the magazine's website in early 2011. "Luckily, Hulu's DramaFever channel had more than 20 more series, and there are thousands of episodes, all subtitled in English, available to watch for free." He went on to say, "K-Dramas can appear simplistic and downright campy to an American viewer, but they're also fascinating and weirdly comforting in a 'movie-of-the-week' kind of way," Lee said. "They're not afraid to whack you over the head with an important moral lesson or social critique."

The growing popularity of Korean dramas is represented in a slew of websites designed for their viewing. Aside from YouTube and Hulu, this also includes smaller online destinations like Drama Fever, Drama Crazy, Viki, and My Soju.

Soompi Finds a Niche with Drama Content

If Korean drama fans have anything in common with wine lovers, it's that they seem to enjoy reading about their favorite shows as much as actually watching them. Soompi, Drama Beans, Korea.com, and Withs.com appear to be the most popular among the growing assortment of online destinations where people discuss all things related to Korean dramas. Each of these websites doubles as a media destination and online community as the creators and readers work together to produce a wealth of content, including recaps and reviews as well as video excerpts and English subtitles.

Soompi, which was recently acquired by the Korean Internet technology firm Enswers, has established itself as the leader of the pack. The website has more than a million login subscribers alone and continues to see its traffic growing rapidly since drawing more than 51 million visitors in 2010. Its users are very active, with ongoing offline meet-ups in some 50 countries around the world.

Lee Young-ae fan club on Soompi

Chapter Two

WHY **K-DRAMA?**

The Appeal of K-Drama

Stars like Bae Yong-joon and Lee Young-ae personify the Korean drama frenzy that is now spreading beyond the Asia-Pacific region, but a closer look into the phenomenon shows that it has been about more than just pretty faces. In fact, it could be argued that the shows have made the stars, not the other way around.

Granted, getting Bae could be all it takes to sell a soap opera to audiences in Japan, China, and other Asian countries, where Hallyu has been a decade-long fever. The growing reception enjoyed by the dramas in other regions like North America, Europe, and the Middle East, however, indicates a universal appeal that transcends different cultural boundaries.

The underlying story behind the worldwide ripple effect generated by Korean dramas is that they have provided what amounts to safe, middle-of-the-road entertainment, while mixing in enough sugary, romantic plots and social mobility angles to keep viewers emotionally invested. Many loyal foreign fans of Korean soap operas talk about their affection for "Korean-style" romances and fuzzy, feel-good stories, and most of their comments on online message boards seem to be about storylines and writing rather than actors and actresses.

Family-Based Confucian Values

Many Korean dramas deal with the country's traditional values in familial relationships, which strikes a chord with Asian viewers who share the cultural affinity and makes them reliable family entertainment in other parts of the world.

Fan Hong, a professor at Tsinghua University's School of Journalism and Communication, believes that Korean dramas have the power to appeal to global audiences because *jeong*—a Korean term for human affection—is usually a central theme. "Korean dramas deal with everyday life and familiar subjects, and thus many Chinese people favor Korean dramas for their human codes," she explained at a 2005 seminar. "In particular, their main themes are mostly friendship, family values, and love, which are universal feelings that appeal to a wide audience. This factor can provide an important connection with people in other parts of the world as well as China."

Hong also pointed out that the storytelling of Korean dramas conveys a uniquely "Korean spirit," blending traditional values of Confucianism with Western materialism and individualism, which registers with the modern audience. Older viewers can relate to the traditional values emphasized in the dramas—family relationships, respect for parents, and love between

The family of *Boys Over Flowers* protagonist Geum Jan-di: poor but tight-knit

siblings—which remain common virtues in Asian cultures despite rapid social changes and an influx of Western individualism over the past century.

Less Provocative, More Universal

In addition to having central themes of love, family life, and friendship, Korean dramas are less sexual and violent than the products coming from Hollywood. This allows them to reach a wider age range and achieve a borderless appeal that resonates in more conservative parts of the world such as the Middle East.

Interestingly, the ability to tell a love story without using sexualized images appears to be an important reason that Korean dramas are

Autumn in My Heart was tremendously popular in Asia and Europe with its depiction of innocent love.

winning over more American viewers. Although Korean television dramas are diverse in genre, romance remains king, as evidenced by the global popularity of *Winter Sonata*, *Autumn in My Heart*, and *Stairway to Heaven*. The main purpose of romantic dramas, in Korea or elsewhere, is to leave viewers feeling warm and happy.

The successful Korean dramas, including the ones mentioned above, have avoided being too banal and obvious with creative writing, providing intriguing characters and just enough twists and turns to keep viewers guessing.

Simple Stories with Emotional Power

Korean dramas rarely follow the "season" formats that are the norm for American shows, where networks decide whether or not to renew a series for another year or over a specific time period based on their ratings and revenue. The Korean shows are usually designed to last a specific number of episodes, which makes the narratives more compact and dedicated to a central theme. This contrasts with American shows, where writers are given more freedom to experiment with the storyline due to the flexible duration of the series.

This goes some way in explaining why Korean plots are often more emotionally charged than in the dramas of the West, relying more on dramatizing evolving relationships or conflicts between sensitive individuals than on simply creating and connecting incidents. Viewers from China, Hong Kong, and Taiwan frequently say that their local soap operas aren't as dramatic or emotionally sensitive as Korean ones.

No drama better represents this Korean trait than *Winter Sonata*, which touched off nothing short of a sensation in Japan upon its NHK debut in 2004. The show depicts a young woman and her amnesiac lover against the backdrop of snow-covered forests and lakes; it is mechanically contrived to tell a beautiful, tragic tale and wet a few handkerchiefs. Bae Yong-joon, as the man who can't remember his girlfriend, maintains a sense of melancholy and sadness—and, of course, is all sorts of handsome and gentle. It would have been rare for an American drama to pursue such a storyline without mixing in a steamy scene or two, but *Winter Sonata* managed to do just fine. And Bae's character seemed to represent everything Japanese women wanted in men (minus the car accident and memory loss part).

The *Winter Sonata* effect is clearly reflected in an *Asahi Shimbun* article published on July 2011. The piece stated that "Japanese women now adore men who are gentle and show less aggression in relationships, a type described as 'herbivorous,' as opposed to 'carnivorous' men."

The detailed, often intense depiction of emotional ebb and flow gives Korean dramas an edginess that is not attributable to sensationalism. This gives them a cross-national appeal as cultural exports, allowing their positioning as alternatives to bolder shows from the US, Europe, and Japan. Particularly for viewers in Asia and the Middle East, the Korean culture and sentiments reflected in Hallyu dramas seem to come across as more accessible and acceptable than what is seen in shows made in Hollywood, many of which are awkward for families to watch together. For such viewers, the lives shown in Korean dramas are for the most part plausible and something to be emulated, which can't be said for shows like *Gossip Girl*. Almost every Korean drama, moreover, revolves around characters working their way up from the bottom, which contributes to the shows' global popularity because, well, everyone roots for the underdogs.

In many Asian cities, Korean dramas seem to be influencing lifestyles and consumer behavior, which speaks to their cultural appeal. Many Korean drama fans spend to share the fashion choices of the stylish fictional characters and crave the city life they live.

Korean *Han* Intensifies Drama

Another unique characteristic of Korean dramas is the underlying cultural trait Koreans refer to as *han*. This could be described as a collective sentiment of sorrow, regret, resentment, and, often, yearning for vengeance. This may be a difficult concept for non-Koreans to understand, as the strong emotions are accompanied by a sense of passivity, fueled by fatalism. Some scholars have theorized that *han*, which is considered a universal element of the Korean experience, evolved from the country's historical suffering, including oppressive Japanese colonial rule and the devastation of the Korean War.

It appears that the complexity of *han* isn't keeping foreign viewers from embracing Korean popular culture, as the sentiment has been critical in adding emotional depth to global hits like *Winter Sonata*, *Jewel in the Palace*, and *Autumn in My Heart*. For example, *Jewel in the Palace* reflects the vicissitudes experienced by a female protagonist who overcomes all kinds of odds and discrimination as a woman in a strictly hierarchical society during the Joseon era. The heroine lives with such *han*, but she

Janggeum is unjustly exiled as a result of court intrigues. But she does not despair, sublimating her *han* to achieve a human victory.

uses it as a driving force in taking her life to a new level. The story is reflective of minorities who have been historically marginalized, creating an emotional outlet through dramatic devices and connecting the story with the deep emotions experienced by the characters. These emotional outbursts motivated by *han* draw more sympathy and hope for overcoming adversity and making dreams come true, not only among Korean audiences but foreign ones as well.

Government Support

It would be difficult to deny that the Korean drama boom has been assisted by efforts from the South Korean government to build and sustain the wave. The market for Korean popular culture has grown rapidly since the country adopted a more open stance on cultural imports in the 1990s. Now, the country is looking to exploit the era of globalization with "soft power," converting its pop culture products into export items and promoting a youthful and dynamic image of the country.

The Korean drama boom has gained much of its momentum through government support. The Korean culture industry has grown dramatically since the 1990s, a decade that saw an

© KBS

Winter Sonata

influx of different culture along with a policy of greater openness by the government. Korean dramas also received indirect government support through development of popular culture in the past. Today, however, the government is pushing ahead with more aggressive policies to boost the ongoing Hallyu boom through a variety of channels, including support for short dramas and amendments to laws related to the quality of the drama production environment.

Meanwhile, governmental institutions like the Korean Culture and Information Service and the Korea Foundation are introducing Korean culture in Central and South American countries where it is relatively unknown. The Korea Foundation supports the airing of Korean soap operas free of charge; as a result, *Autumn in My Heart* and *Winter Sonata* were dubbed into Spanish for broadcast in eleven countries, including Mexico, while *Jewel in the Palace* was shown in eight Central and South American countries, including Peru.

Foreign Media Respond to K-Drama

Korean Epics Sweep Iran

The international popularity of Korean dramas has been a subject of interest for media around the world, especially those in countries where the shows have gained significant viewership.

In Iran, the local magazine *Hamshahry Javan* (*Young Citizen*) explored the popularity of *Jumong* and its effects beyond the living room in a 2009 article titled "Korean Movies: Cultural Envoys for Iran." "Korean dramas have storylines that people can easily identify with," the article said, "and the plots and themes are equally easy to follow. There is little complexity to the stories, which makes it easy to distinguish between good and evil roles. Korean dramas are a mixture of history and fables." The popularity of Korean cultural exports has been amplified through online video sites and message boards, according to the article, which put the Internet-using population in Iran at over 23 million.

In attempting to explain the Iranian public's love affair with *Jumong*, the magazine came up with an interesting answer: beautiful costumes. "The costumes in Korean dramas are beautiful, and all of them are brightly colored," it said. "These ancient outfits cover the whole body, which is similar to customs for Iranian women. This makes Iranian women want to buy Korean dresses," The article went on to note, "The key characters are well cast in their roles, and their faces really express what's going on in their minds. In Korean dramas, Iranian people see people with many different characteristics, and through them they can imagine love, hatred, jealousy, sacrifice, and treason."

The state-run Jordanian television network had never shown a foreign series before airing *Jewel in the Palace* during prime time in October 2011.

Jumong star Song Il-gook is greeted by the Iranian press.

The first Korean drama broadcast by Iran's state-run television network was *Jewel in the Palace*, which became one of the country's most watched television shows ever. "Many Iranians could empathize with the female actress Lee Young-ae," the magazine said, "and if you were in Iran, you could see that many people talked about her character and the challenges she faced. Korea is rich in both culture and heritage, and Iran also has a great and ancient history, but not many movies have been produced about its history. People in Eastern countries are known for being more sympathetic emotionally than people in Western countries, and this really shows in the dramas and movies they produce."

"These two countries could have more cultural contact with each other," the article noted, "and Iranian and Korean movies could play the role of cultural envoys. Through cinema, Koreans and Iranians could become more familiar with each other's literature and culture, and this could help to improve bilateral relations. Politicians could also consider these facts and use them as a basis for improving relations between the two countries."

Fast-Growing Indonesian Fan Base

Korean dramas are all the rage in Indonesia as well, as reported by *the Jakarta Post* in its July 2011 article titled "Korean Wave Casts a Spell in Indonesia." As was the case in many other Asian nations, *Winter Sonata* was first to trigger the boom, and a slew of other Korean dramas and movies have aired on Indonesian television since then. "Though these Korean cultural products—mostly popular among girls and middle-aged women—still lagged behind local reality shows in the ratings, they were certainly the most popular among Asian drama series and films," the newspaper said. It also reported that the number of Hallyu fans in Indonesia was growing rapidly, as people developed a greater general interest in Korean language, arts, culture, and food. The Korean community is now the biggest foreign community in Indonesia, with almost 50,000 people, according to the newspaper.

To promote Korean language and culture further and meet the demand for Korean cultural products among Indonesians, the Korean government opened its first Korean Cultural Center in Jakarta in July 2011.

(Left) An article on *Protect the Boss* in an Indonesian newspaper
(Right) *The Jakarta Post* writes about the Hallyu fever in Indonesia.

Economist Pinpoints Reasons for Drama Success

Korea's success in pop culture exports was analyzed by Britain's influential business magazine *The Economist*, which claimed that the family-friendly,

Confucian themes typical of Korean dramas appeal more to Asians than Western dramas do. "By their rags-to-riches storylines these dramas are able to speak directly to audiences who have lived the Asian economic boom of the past two decades," Michael Shin of Cornell University argues in the 2010 article.

The fact that so many viewers are captivated by characters who often ditch their monotonous middle-class jobs in pursuit of greatness perhaps indicates that many Asians feel dissatisfied with their careers despite the prosperity that has come with growth, *The Economist* suggests. The first hints of Hallyu came just after Korea's economy collapsed during the 1998 financial crisis in Asia; in the decade that followed, three administrations looked to pop culture products as a tool of soft power, the magazine observed.

New York Times Covers K-Drama Popularity

The New York Times was one of earliest US media outlets to recognize what Hallyu was on the verge of becoming. In a 2005 article, the newspaper observed that the increasing popularity of Korean dramas was injecting new confidence into the country's efforts to foster its cultural products as an export force. It cited the frenzy for *Jewel in the Palace* in Hong Kong, Taiwan, and such unexpected places as Mongolia, as well as

(Clockwise from top left) *Stairway to Heaven*; *Lovers in Paris*; Yoon Eun-hye alongside Sarah Jessica Parker at a cosmetics promotional event in Shanghai; *Gourmet* poster and menu at the entrance of Seorabeol, a Korean restaurant in Hong Kong. The restaurant drew attention with a special *Gourmet* menu after the show's popularity.

the success of *Winter Sonata* in Japan and Uzbekistan; *Autumn in My Heart* in Thailand and Malaysia; and *Lovers in Paris* in Vietnam. "In China, South Korean dramas are sold, and pirated, everywhere, and the young adopt the clothing and hairstyles made cool by South Korean stars," the article said. "South Korea, historically more worried about fending off cultural domination by China and Japan than spreading its own culture abroad, is emerging as the pop culture leader of Asia."

The newspaper noted that the value of Korea's entertainment industry, which began attracting heavy government investment only in the late 1990s, jumped from $8.5 billion in 1999 to $43.5 billion in 2003. In 2003, the country exported $650 million in cultural products; the amount had been so insignificant before 1998 that the government could not provide figures. "But the figures tell only part of the story," the newspaper said. "The booming South Korean presence on television and in the movies has led Asians to buy up South Korean goods and to travel to South Korea, traditionally not a popular tourist destination. The images that Asians traditionally have associated with the country—violent student marches, the Demilitarized Zone, division—have given way to trendy entertainers and new technology."

Financial Times Cites
Pure Love as Factor in K-Drama Success

In December 2004, the *Financial Times* published an article titled "South Korea's soppy soaps win hearts across Asia." It explained that as part of Hallyu's influence across Asia, tear-jerking soaps such as *Winter Sonata* were giving Korea a new reputation and boosting tourism revenues, as well as providing something of an escape from reality. "These soaps, which also include *Autumn in My Heart* and *Love Story in Harvard*, have a common theme: beating the odds to find true love and happiness," the newspaper said. "But unlike their Western counterparts, there is no sex or even lust in these dramas." It determined that the "right mix of fantasy and reality" was behind the dramas' international success.

Foreign Faces in K-Drama

As Korea has become economically powerful outwardly and multicultural inwardly in recent years, it has experienced a significant increase in the number of foreign residents and appears to be in the midst of a transition toward a multiethnic society.

American Daniel Henney

These important social changes are beginning to show in Korean dramas, where the stars are no longer only limited to Koreans; they also include appealing foreigners with a fluent command of Korean. Korean dramas are set in exotic overseas locales, and the period pieces feature not only ancient history dating back to before the Joseon era but also the modern period after Western cultural influences set in on Korean soil.

American Daniel Henney, who cut his teeth as a fashion model in the US, shot to stardom with *My Lovely Samsoon* in 2005 and has since appeared in numerous dramas and movies like *Spring Waltz*, *The Fugitive*: *Plan B*, and *My Father*. His pan-Asian popularity has been landing him opportunities in Hollywood, as he appeared in the movie *X-Men Origins*: *Wolverine* and the CBS television drama *Three Rivers*.

American Dennis Oh appeared in *Sweet Spy* and *East of Eden*, while

Americans Sean Richard and Ricky Kim worked together in both *Jejungwon* and *Athena: Goddess of War*. French Julien Kang rose to stardom with the MBC sitcom *Highkick 2* and has landed more serious roles in dramas like *Road Number One*. He currently appears on the MBC sitcom *Highkick 3* as an English teacher who loves Korean food and culture.

On MBC's *Royal Family*, American actor Peter Holman shone in a supporting role. Even before his television debut, movie buffs recognized him from his appearance in films like *He's on Duty* and *The Case of Itaewon Homicide*.

New Zealand-born Kevin Were, whose day job is as a university English professor, is best known for his role as a movie director in *Secret Garden*, although he also appeared in *Royal Family* and *My Princess*.

American Michael Blunck became a household name after portraying an American Buddhist monk in MBC's *Bibimbap of Jewels* and appearing in SBS's *New Tales of Gisaeng*.

Pierre Deporte, a French actor who even has a Korean name (Hwang Chan-bin), played the lead role of a shipwrecked Englishman who finds himself on 17th century Jeju Island in MBC's 2009 drama *Tamra, the Island*.

Frenchman Pierre Deporte

Chapter Three

HISTORY OF
K-DRAMA

Twenty years after the British Broadcasting Corporation (BBC) started airing in 1936, the era of Korean television broadcasting began in May 1956 with the establishment of HLKZ-TV. This small experimental network would later become part of KBS. At the time, people in Korea stared admiringly at the television sets on display at Hwashin Department Store. But HLKZ-TV would be shut down by an unfortunate fire. Finally, the Korean Broadcasting System (KBS), the nation's first public broadcaster, went on air in December 31, 1961, ushering in a new era of Korean dramas.

It wasn't until the early 1960s that television networks began airing dramas regularly. But there were nothing like the major family entertainment that dramas have become today; the distribution of televisions was still low, and the content of the shows was heavily

The drama *Assi* was hugely popular in the 1970s. It portrayed a typically self-sacrificial Korean woman living through a turbulent time in history.

controlled by the military government. However, dramas started to become a more essential part of daily television programming after the government lifted a ban in 1969 that prevented broadcasters from gaining commercial revenue from advertisers. Competition for viewers commenced, and this had television networks investing more serious efforts into producing and promoting their shows.

The early 1970s marked a heyday for television dramas, with the three broadcasters TBC, KBS and MBC airing about 15 a day. The boom was somewhat subdued, however, after the heavy-handed government began imposing sterner controls over content "in poor taste" and requiring networks to allocate more of their broadcasting hours to news and educational programming.

The popularity of dramas reached another level between the mid-1980s and early 1990s, when broadcasters began tailoring their shows to the younger audience, offering "trendy" dramas that focused on the lives and loves of young people. These were influenced by the programs shown on Japanese television networks. The emergence of pay television platforms like cable and satellite in the mid-1990s gave dramas another jolt by expanding the market for entertainment content and intensifying competition for viewers.

As noted above, the consumption of Korean dramas has become international in the current era, defined as it is by globalization and the ubiquity of the Internet. Geographical boundaries of cultural influence continue to become blurred. Although Korean dramas come in various forms and styles, the most internationally popular have belonged to the genres of romance, romantic comedy, and period drama.

1960s: The Age of Enlightenment

During the 1960s, two commercial networks—TBC (Tong Yang Television Company) and MBC (Munhwa Broadcasting Company)—were founded to complement state-run KBS. This is also when television dramas began shaping their early formats and content. Through the mid-1960s, however, most dramas were made with the purpose of "educating" the public and massaging the egos of the authoritarian government. For example, the

The KBS building in the 1960s

AFKN:
Providing of Variety of Foreign Culture to Korea until the 1980s

One year after Korea's first broadcasting network went on the air on May 12, 1956, with the start of HLKZ-TV, the commercially operated AFKN-TV—an affiliate of the American Forces Radio and Television Service and the second largest of five networks managed by the Army Broadcasting Service—began service. Although the target audiences for AFKN-TV were US military personnel, civilian employees, and residents of South Korea, its impact was huge, delivering foreign culture into the living rooms of ordinary Korean viewers.

AFKN-TV played a significant role for many young Koreans. The size of the Korean "shadow audience" for AFKN-TV was enormous—so many ordinary viewers watched it that all Korean newspapers and most television guides carried AFKN-TV listings alongside their Korean program schedules.

Many Korean viewers encountered Western culture as they watched AFKN-TV for purposes of entertainment and even education. In his 2007 book *An AFKN Kid's Looking into the United States*, MBC reporter Yoo Jae-yong confessed that he learned English by watching *Sesame Street* and *Ryan's Hope*. World- famous film director Bong Joon-ho (renowned for *The Host*) was also a big fan of the foreign movies aired at night through AFKN-TV when he was young, although he couldn't fully understand the scripts. Many other people watched AFKN-TV shows that were more advanced, freer, and fresher than the Korean productions of the day, an experience that allowed them to encounter a variety of foreign culture.

country's very first drama series, *Backstreet of Seoul*, which aired on KBS in 1962, was more of a lecture on the problems of urban life than a meaningful attempt at family entertainment. *Yeong-i's Diary*, a KBS children's drama that aired in 1970, often seemed like a platform for public campaign announcements. And *Real Theater*, a KBS drama that aired for two decades between 1964 and 1985, was a major tool in the government's anti-communism drive.

Injecting some creative input into the television drama scene was TBC, which remained a major competitor of KBS until it was absorbed by the public broadcaster in 1980. TBC was more aggressive than its rivals in employing entertainment-oriented programming; its dramas even touched on then-taboo subjects like infidelity, which had viewers divided on how to react.

1970s: Entering the Era of True Entertainment

The influence of television broadcasting increased dramatically during the 1970s as more and more households acquired their own television sets. This was also the era when soap operas began to overtake movies as the definitive platform for video entertainment.

Drama storylines were soppier than they had been in the 1960s and inspired more by everyday life and incidents than by political agendas. The plots of the 1970 TBC drama *Assi* and the 1972 KBS hit *Yeoro* were built around characters enduring difficult lives. These shows were set against the backdrop of Korea's turbulent history since the latter part of the Japanese colonial rule and the Korean War between 1950 and 1953. The TBC show *Reed* portrayed the lives of people enduring extreme poverty.

The 1970s were also a time when a number of long-running dramas began cementing their case as all-time classics. The MBC show *Susa Banjang* (*Chief Detective*)—which could be described as a less flashy Korean equivalent of *Starsky and Hutch*—was a consistently popular show throughout its run from 1971 to 1989. It could be said that the evolution of drama storylines mirrored real-world changes during those 20 years. In the earlier days of the drama, *Susa Banjang's* writers had their characters primarily occupied with crimes related to poverty. However, more serious and violent criminals like drug dealers, robbers, kidnappers, and murderers were frequently featured in episodes during the 1980s, when these types of social problems were actually on the rise. *Susa Banjang's* lengthy run came to an end in 1989.

1980s: Portraits of a Modern Korea

Color television was introduced into Korean living rooms in the 1980s, which was when dramas began showing more diversified colors as well. In 1980, period dramas such as *Founding the Country* and *500 Years*

(Left) *Plum Blossoms in Snow* from the series *500 Years of Joseon Kingdom*
(Right) *Susa Banjang*

of *Joseon Kingdom* told the tales of heroic leaders based on a liberal interpretation of historical facts. Meanwhile, the MBC show *Pastoral Diary* and the KBS show *Hill of the Rising Sun* depicted the lives of people in small farming villages. Their aim was to evoke affection and nostalgia from viewers who were witnessing the country's rapid urbanization process. Kim Su-hyun, who remains Korea's most sought-after drama writer, had her first major breakthrough in 1986 with the MBC series *Love and Ambition*, which many consider the country's defining drama of the 1980s.

1990s: More Ideas, Better Results

The 1990s were a period of a technological change in the Korean broadcasting industry, which saw broadcast media becoming even more important than in the past. During these years, the Korean broadcasting industry utilized new technological developments such as satellite technology and interactive cable systems, which allowed Korea to participate fully in the information society. Furthermore, the licensing of new terrestrial broadcaster SBS in 1990 triggered a renewed ratings battle

(Left) *Love and Ambition* (Center) *Pastoral Diary* (Right) *Hoecheonmun* from the series *500 Years of Joseon Kingdom*

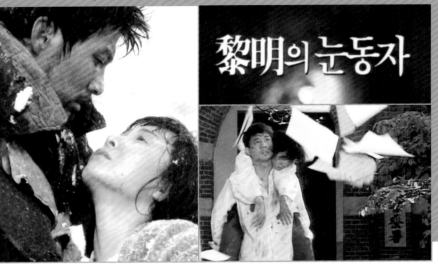

Eyes of Dawn was truly a landmark show as the first blockbuster series in Korean drama history.

in the television industry. This led to networks investing more money and effort into dramas and other entertainment.

Eyes of Dawn, which aired from 1991 to 1992, was truly a landmark show as the first blockbuster series in Korean drama history. It depicted the vicissitudes of Korean history from the colonial period (1910-45) to the Korean War (1950-53), pouring some 200 million won into the production of each episode. The drama attempted such innovations as pre-production and overseas locations in 1991 and drew rave reviews from both audiences and critics for its solid script and the good performances of such veteran actors as Chae Si-ra and Choi Jae-sung.

The competition only intensified as Korea entered the pay television era in 1996 with the debut of cable television. This significantly boosted the demand for entertainment content and further motivated the creators of dramas to provide something bigger, bolder, and better.

The genre of trendy dramas that relied on smart dialogue and visual appeal reached a new peak during the 1990s. The most successful of them was MBC's 1994 hit *Jealousy*, a romantic drama starring Choi Su-jong and Choi Jin-sil. For the younger generation of viewers, trendy dramas represented a welcome departure from the tear-jerking melodramas that had previously dominated prime time slots. They appreciated shows like *Jealousy* for their young characters and their stylish and realistic descriptions of urban life. The show's soundtrack was also a massive hit on the record charts, which inspired broadcasters to think more about linking the popularity of their dramas with merchandise sales.

Meanwhile, the 1990s saw the production of more diverse shows with the relaxation of governmental regulations and censorship. No television network benefited more from the newfound creative freedom than the brand new SBS, which singlehandedly rewrote the history of Korean television entertainment with its iconic 1995 miniseries *Sandglass*. Starring the A-list trio of Choi Min-soo, Ko Hyun-jung, and Park Sang-won, this show captivated viewers with its daring depiction of life and oppression under politically hard times. It remains one of the highest-rated dramas in Korean history, averaging a 50.8 percent audience share

Jealousy

through its 24 episodes and a staggering 64.3 percent share for the series finale.

A notable part of *Sandglass* was its recreation of the 1980 Gwangju Uprising, which took up two episodes. Hundreds of civilians were killed in the southwestern city when the military regime dispatched paratroopers to crush a democratization protest. The incident, which has since been renamed the "Gwangju Democratization Movement," is seen as one of the darkest moments of Korea's post-war history.

Prior to *Sandglass*, the Gwangju Uprising had been largely avoided as a subject for popular culture. The drama's huge success was followed by a slew of films dealing with the tragedy, including *The Petal* (1996), *Peppermint Candy* (2000), and *May 18* (2007).

(Left) *Sandglass* was an event that had even men glued to their TV sets, even though they were not known for watching dramas at the time of airing. (Right) *Sandglass* was the first drama to address the tragic Gwangju Uprising.

Power Shift: From TV to Smartphones

As recently as a few years ago, you could ask someone how they watch television dramas and be told, "Half-lying on the couch," or "While eating dinner." This no longer applies in the information and technology era. More people are choosing to watch TV through devices such as smartphones and tablet computers, a situation that is bringing about a power shift in the industry.

The phenomenon can be seen in the activities of tech-savvy fans. When *Secret Garden* made it big in the early 2011, a related smartphone application was made available both at Apple's App Store and the Android Market. Featuring previews and clips from the drama, the application was downloaded more than 60,000 times right after the drama came to an end.

NHN, Korea's leading portal company, launched the application "Jang Keunsuk Lite" on October 19, 2011. This came in response to Jang's ever-deepening popularity in Asia. The service will be provided in four languages—Japanese, English, Korean, and Chinese—as a way of communicating with Jang's worldwide fans.

In Japan, the first Hallyu drama application, *Dream High* (starring members of the boy band 2PM), was launched for iPhone and iPad users in July 2011. The application consists of a 35-minute video with music, dance performances, and photographs used in the drama.

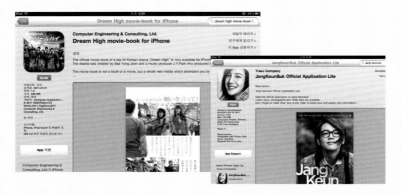

(Left) *My Girlfriend is a Nine-Tailed Fox*
(Right) DVD Box of *You're Beautiful*

2000s to the Present: K-Drama Goes Global

The rapid advancement in information and communication technologies in recent years has opened a new and exciting chapter for Korean dramas. The growth of online video services and the emergence of social networking on the Internet meant that shows aired on KBS, MBC, and SBS were watched, shared, and dissected by a much larger audience than just Koreans. Facing this international change, the Korean television industry responded in the only way it could—by attempting to rise to the challenge and spending massively to do its best impersonations of Hollywood.

Romantic dramas were now filmed in some of the world's most beautiful and awe-inspiring locations—from Paris to Tahiti—to go with their pretty people and flashy clothes. And an enormous amount of money was injected into the emerging genre of action-adventure dramas such as *Iris*

(Clockwise from top left)
Sungkyunkwan Scandal,
Athena: Goddess of War,
Lovers in Paris

and *Athena: Goddess of War*, which aimed to intoxicate viewers with the Michael Bay recipe of explosions, gun fights, and car chases.

Period dramas enjoyed a renaissance in the new millennium, winning over a new generation of viewers by marrying their historically inspired material with advanced filming techniques, better writing, and massive action sequences. *Jewel in the Palace* was obviously the game changer, while *Heo Jun*, *Founder Wang Geon*, and *Jumong* garnered high ratings as well. And the storylines no longer revolved around just kings, palace life, and wars. The KBS series *The Slave Hunters*, an action-adventure series about runaway slaves, bounty hunters, and fallen aristocrats, was one of the most widely watched dramas of 2010.

Japanese Popular Culture in Korea

During the Japanese colonial period (1910-45), Koreans couldn't use their mother tongue or receive adequate Korean education. Against this backdrop, subsequent Korean governments took a strict position against Japanese culture. For a long time, governments banned the importation of Japanese popular cultural products into Korea in the interests of Korean cultural independence.

In April 1998, then President Kim Dae-jung pushed for a gradual opening of the domestic market to Japanese popular culture. "We are not afraid of accepting Japanese popular culture," he said, "as we have historically accepted foreign cultures and recreated them in our own culture. The same is true for Japanese culture." On November 20 of that year, the Korean government announced a gradual opening to Japanese culture in three phases: Japanese films, publications, and animation.

This opening had its principal impact on the Korean drama scene, which at that time dealt mainly with serious (and monotonous) themes. The dramas were infused with Japanese-inspired comical and light-hearted subject matter, which constituted the main elements in youth dramas and romantic comedies. Also, many of the Korean soap operas were based on Japanese manga, reinterpreted to suit the Korean situation. These enjoyed enormous popularity both at home and abroad.

A case in point is *Boys Over Flowers*, which also enjoyed great popularity in its Japanese and Taiwanese incarnations. This show had a nuanced difference from the Japanese version in that the characters and stories reflected Korea's unique sentiments. In the Japanese version, a female protagonist born into a poor and incompetent family enters a high-end private school because of her parents' vanity and overcomes difficulty with her indomitable spirit. In the Korean version, the heroine is still the child of a humble family, but this time is a swimmer at a school without a pool. One day, she accidently saves a student who falls into the pool at a prestigious private school, and her actions get her admitted into the school.

The Korean version added the "swimming" element, which was not present in the original. It also offered a different development of the storyline as it presented the story of the heroine overcoming a harsh reality. The setting added more dramatic flavor to the original content, which had merely empowered the character with her personal undauntedness. In this version,

The popular Japanese manga *Boys Over Flowers*

emphasis was placed on her self-fulfillment as she pursues her own destiny through talent and effort. This, along with other entertaining elements, was another factor in the drama's enthusiastic reception in other Asian countries.

The Korean version of *Boys Over Flowers* was beloved by fans all over Asia.

© KBS

Chapter Four

TOP K-DRAMAS AND **STARS**

Top 10 K-Dramas

Romantic melodramas, romantic comedies, and period pieces stand as the three main genres of Korean dramas. While series like *Autumn in My Heart* opened up the golden age of romantic dramas, they now appear to be conceding a large chunk of the prime time slots to comedies and historical dramas, which are also consistently finding audiences overseas.

The biggest romantic comedy hits have been *My Lovely Samsoon*, *My Princess*, *Palace*, and *The Greatest Love*. Another thing to consider is that intensified competition over ratings has more and more shows relying on non-specialist actors, like pop stars or supermodels, whose acting limitations are better hidden in romantic comedies than in emotionally

© KBS

charged melodramas along the lines of *Winter Sonata*.

Period pieces have always been a big part of Korean prime time television, and their popularity is showing no signs of waning a decade into the 21st century. As seen with *Jewel in the Palace*, these dramas are deftly incorporating exotic elements of times gone by with every aspect of the world outside the television screen: life, death, love, hate, hope, disappointment, loss, and redemption. Period dramas have mostly told the stories of prominent historical figures like kings and legendary warriors, but since the success of *Jewel in the Palace*, an increasing number of shows have been built around characters from lower social backgrounds, as seen in *Hwang Jin-i* and *The Slave Hunters*.

The ten Korean dramas introduced below have been particularly beloved by foreign fans, generating buzz not only in Korea but also in other countries since the Hallyu phenomenon began its reign in Asia and beyond in the 2000s.

Jewel in the Palace (2003-2004)

Jewel in the Palace (*Daejanggeum*) is one of the watershed dramas that rewrote the Korean historic drama genre. It was the work of veteran director Lee Byung-hoon, who received great acclaim for both the popularity and the dramatic quality of his work directing such dramas as *Amhaengeosa* (*Secret Royal Inspector*) and *Heo Jun*. Lee showed his talent by making even evil characters seem sympathetic to the public with delicate, psychologically sophisticated portrayals and spectacular suspense sequences based in solid storytelling in *Jewel in the Palace*. This series enjoyed a strong reception at home, with a 58 percent audience share, before airing in other countries.

The drama shines with its main character Janggeum. This figure actually did appear in the *Annals of the Joseon Kingdom*, but only in the brief account of "a female physician who was particularly favored by King Jungjong." Using an actual figure from history as his basis, Lee Byung-hoon applied his fictional imagination in shedding new light on a female role that was overshadowed in male-oriented historical accounts. The drama depicts the human victory of a woman overcoming handicaps and obstacles, pioneering her own life in the face of a male-centered Neo-Confucian social hierarchy without losing her identity. The series was very popular for its inspirational story.

Winter Sonata (2002)

First broadcast in Korea in 2002, *Winter Sonata* was the biggest global hit in the four-part *Endless Love* drama series directed by Yoon Seok-ho and aired by KBS. (The other parts were *Autumn in My Heart*, *Summer Scent*, and *Spring Waltz*.)

The drama portrays the loves and sorrows of four people who have been friends since high school: Jeong Yu-jin (Choi Ji-woo), Gang Jun-sang (Bae Yong-joon), Kim Sang-hyeok (the late Park Yong-ha), and Oh Chae-rin (Bak Sol-mi). Jun-sang and Yu-jin were each other's first loves, but their relationship is cut short after Jun-sang is injured in a car accident and loses his memory due to brain damage. His mother decides to have him brainwashed by a psychologist so he will not remember his painful childhood as an illegitimate son. She then moves to the US with Jun-sang, who starts a new life under the identity of Lee Min-hyeong, while his friends are left to believe he is dead. Ten years later, Yu-jin, now working as an interior designer, is in a relationship with Sang-hyeok. During a business meeting, she encounters Min-hyeong, who has returned from the US as an established architect, which prompts her to put off her engagement to Sang-hyeok.

© KBS

© KBS

Autumn in My Heart (2000)

Autumn in My Heart was the first installment of director Yoon Seok-ho's four-part *Endless Love* series and his second most successful work behind *Winter Sonata*. Yoon has always been unapologetic about his determination to leave viewers misty-eyed, and *Autumn in My Heart* speaks to his unique talent for making over-the-top tearjerkers seem understated. As with *Winter Sonata*, *Autumn in My Heart* attempts to tell a beautiful, tragic tale through beautiful people against the backdrop of beautiful scenery.

Jun-seo (Song Seung-heon) and Eun-seo (Song Hye-kyo) grow up as siblings. But then Eun-seo is hit by a truck, and blood tests at the hospital reveal that she was accidentally switched with another girl at birth. The two daughters are eventually returned to their biological parents—Eun-seo is reunited with her widowed mother, and her childhood rival Shin-ae moves in with Jun-seo's family. Years go by, during which time Jun-seo's family goes to the US. Jun-seo eventually returns to Korea as a successful artist and encounters Eun-seo, who is working at a hotel as a maid. By this time, Eun-seo is the love of Tae-seok (Won Bin), a son from a wealthy family who happens to be an old friend of Jun-seo. Eun-seo and Jun-seo continue to meet as siblings but become emotionally confused after beginning to develop feelings for each other.

Sarangbi:
Winter Sonata Director Meets New Hallyu Star

Jang Keun-suk, a next generation Hallyu star in Japan, and *Winter Sonata* director Yoon Seok-ho will be coming together for the new television drama *Sarangbi*. Expected to air in the first half of 2012, the new series is also the first collaboration in a decade between Yoon and writer Oh Soo-yeon, who created *Winter Sonata*, *Autumn in My Heart*, and *Spring Waltz*. The drama will focus on the essence of love in the 1970s and in 21st century Korea. Jang will play the double role of Seo In-ha, an art student in the 1970s, and Seo's son in present-day Korea, a free-spirited photographer.

Yoona of the K-pop band Girls' Generation will be playing opposite Jang. She will also be tackling a double role, playing Kim Yun-hee in the 1970s and Kim's daughter Yu-ri in present-day Korea. The story sees Yu-ri falling in love with Seo In-ha, played by Jang.

The drama is expected to draw much attention from the public as the first collaboration between Jang and Yoon.

My Lovely Samsoon (2005)

"우리 연애 하는 척 한번 해볼까요?"

The 2005 *My Lovely Samsoon* is a romantic comedy that generated huge ratings and created the so-called "Samsoon syndrome." The romantic comedy touched off a massive sensation that grew with every episode, elevating the main cast members to the most sought-after stars in the Korean entertainment business.

The drama resonated with many average Korean female viewers by featuring an unusual type for the genre: a plump single woman. Starring popular actress Kim Sun-ah and male heartthrobs Hyun Bin and Daniel Henney, the drama lived up to the massive anticipation built up with reports of Kim's struggles to put on weight (à la Renee Zellweger before *Bridget Jones's Diary*) to portray the chubby lead character Sam-soon.

The drama revolves around Sam-soon, a single woman in her early 30s who is insecure about her professional future and worried about her weight. A Cordon Bleu-educated pastry chef, she is eventually hired at a French restaurant owned by Jin-heon. The two of them get off to an awkward start but begin to develop a partnership out of convenience. When Sam-soon finds herself in need of quick money, she agrees to act as Jin-heon's pretend girlfriend so that he can avoid his pushy mother and her blind-date arrangements. The fake relationship slowly turns into genuine affection, but the situation gets complicated when Jin-heon's ex-girlfriend returns from the US—just around the time when Sam-soon's ex-boyfriend comes back into play.

Jumong (2006-2007)

Jumong, an MBC historical drama that aired between May 2006 and March 2007, portrays the life of Jumong Taewang, the founder of the ancient kingdom of Goguryeo (37 BC- 668 AD). A collaboration between the creators of hit period pieces like *Damo* and *Heojun*, *Jumong* was hotly anticipated long before the airing of its first episode, and managed to live up to the hype with its blend of humor, high drama, and action.

Jumong enjoyed high ratings in Korea throughout its run and extended the international popularity of Korean period dramas that started with *Jewel in the Palace*, reaching viewers across Asia and in a number of nations in the Middle East. Song Il-guk, who played *Jumong*, and Han Hye-jin, who took the role of *Jumong*'s wife and future queen So Seon-no, have since become household names.

Very few historical details remain on the life of Jumong before he became king, aside from a myth in the 12th century volume *Samguk Sagi* (*History of the Three Kingdoms*) stating that he was born from an egg conceived between King Geumwa of Dongbuyeo and Yuhwa, the daughter of a river god. Thus, the drama depended almost entirely on the imagination of its writers, who replaced the mythical tales with a down-to-earth storyline about a cowardly prince learning to embrace his potential and eventually establishing his own kingdom that exceeds the legacy of his father.

Coffee Prince (2007)

Based on the novel *The first Shop of Coffee Prince*, this MBC television series tells of the loves and lives of a group of friends working together at a coffee shop. The drama created a phenomenon, generating many spinoff effects. *Coffee Prince* is far from realistic, and its fantastic, cartoonish, and colorful characters dealing with comic circumstances make for a light and cheerful story. Hit dramas have often showcased new social trends, from fashion items to dating styles, and *Coffee Prince* was followed by a new trend of specialty coffee shops on almost every street corner, distinguishing themselves from mega-chains like Starbucks.

Eun-chan (Yun Eun-hye) is a 24-year-old who takes up any job she can find to support her struggling family. Han-gyeol (Gong Yoo) comes from a rich family that owns a food business, but he has no interest in taking over the family trade. The two develop a quick friendship as Han-gyeol mistakes the tomboyish Eun-chan for a man. Not knowing that Eun-chan is actually a girl, Han-gyeol pays her to fake a "gay" relationship with him to fend off his persistent grandmother. Han-gyeol later takes over a rundown coffee shop, renames it "Coffee Prince," and decides to hire only good-looking male employees to attract more female customers.

Full House (2004)

This KBS romantic comedy solidified Song Hye-kyo's status as a megastar and added to the acting credentials of Rain, who cut his showbiz teeth as a singer.

Based on a popular comic book series of the same name, *Full House* managed 30 percent-plus ratings for most of its 16 episodes aired in Korea, and later shone as a television export.

The drama was a huge success, becoming one of the most popular dramas in the Korean cultural expansion known as Hallyu for the sweet and cartoonish touches found in its fictional situations.

The story revolves around Han Ji-eun (Song), a script writer who lives in a house (the "Full House" of the title) built by her father. One day, two of Ji-eun's best friends trick her into believing she has won a free vacation and sell the house while she is gone. Meanwhile, unassuming Ji-eun spots Lee Young-jae (Rain), a superstar actor, on the plane. Little does she know that he bought the house she had no intention of selling. The comedy arises when Ji-eun returns to the house to find it no longer belongs to her. Desperate to buy the house back, she reluctantly agrees to work as Young-jae's maid, struggling to deal with his temper and disorganized lifestyle.

© KBS

© KBS

Boys Over Flowers (2009)

This romantic comedy is based on an eponymous Japanese manga series that was consistently popular throughout its eleven-year run. The KBS version was the fifth television adaptation of the manga, following earlier works in Japan and Taiwan. The drama was one popular at home and abroad for its unique interpretation, infusing Korean sentiments into the original storyline to adjust for cultural differences between Japan and Korea, and casting good-looking new actors who shot to stardom thanks to their roles in it.

Shinhwa High School is a school for rich folk. But Geum Jan-di (Gu Hye-seon), a girl from a poor family, makes it in after saving a boy from jumping off the school's roof during a laundry delivery, an act that is rewarded with a scholarship. Jan-di soon becomes the target of a group of good-looking boys who call themselves the "F4." The gang of four, led by Goo Jun-pyo (I Min-ho), the heir of the family-owned Shinhwa Group, is practically worshiped by the rest of the school, but Jan-di couldn't care less. The plot intensifies as Jun-pyo and Jan-di fall for each other, while the presence of Ji-hoo (Gim Hyeon-jung) starts to make things complicated.

Iris (2009)

This blockbuster spy series hurled a bunch of high-profile stars, including Lee Byung-hun, Kim Tae-hee, Jung Jun-ho, and immensely popular Big Bang singer T.O.P., into a slam-bang mixture of huge explosions, firepower, and high drama.

The show provides a convincing enough plot to justify the shock and awe. It was filmed in various locations in Korea and abroad, including Japan's Akita Prefecture, Budapest, and Shanghai, although most of the action scenes were shot in Seoul, including the climactic gun fight in the bustling streets of Gwanghwamun. The success of the series led to 2010 spinoff *Athena*: *Goddess of War*, which shares the original's record of being the most expensive Korean drama ever made.

The plot revolves around two friends, Kim Hyun-jun (Lee Byung-hun) and Jin Sa-woo (Jung Joon-ho), who trained together as Special Forces soldiers. They are recruited into a secret Korean black ops agency known as the National Security Service (NSS). Their loyalties are tested when they find themselves at the center of an international conspiracy that involves North Korea, global terrorist organizations, and nuclear weapons. Telling of the love, hatred, and betrayals among spies from North and South Korea, the series offered eye-popping spectacles of realistic action, explosions, and gunfights, together with character tensions and mellow romance.

Secret Garden (2010-2011)

This SBS drama starring Hyun Bin and Ha Ji-won was an immediate sensation in Korea, cementing Hyun's status as one of the country's most coveted acting talents. Hyun will have to wait a while to fully cash in on his scorching popularity, though, as he is currently in the middle of a 21-month term in the military, which is compulsory for able-bodied Korean men.

Secret Garden enjoyed massive ratings in Korea and is showing signs of becoming the country's next big television export, as evidenced by strong viewership ratings in the Philippines when it aired on the network GMA in May 2011.

The drama could be described as a 21st century version of *Cinderella* with an extra touch of magic. The main characters are Kim Joo-won (Hyun Bin), an arrogant department store CEO, and Gil Ra-im (Ha Ji-won), a movie stuntwoman in a precarious financial situation. They accidentally meet when Joo-won mistakes Ra-im for a certain A-list actress. This marks the beginning of a bumpy, up-and-down relationship. Joo-won is unsure what to think about his growing affection for Ra-im; complicating matters further is a strange sequence of events that results in them swapping bodies.

Korea Tourism Rush

More and more Korean dramas are becoming international hits, and this means more Korean filming locations are becoming favored landmarks for enthusiastic groups of travelers from Asia and beyond.

No place has benefited more from this television-induced tourism than Nami Island, which quickly emerged from relative anonymity to become a major tourist destination after providing the scenery for *Winter Sonata*. The country's capital city of Seoul, the mountainous Gangwon Province region, and the southernmost resort island of Jeju—traditionally the most popular filming locations—are enjoying a boost in tourism as well.

Nami Island (*Winter Sonata*)

Nami Island, located in a lake near Chuncheon, Gangwon Province, now doubles as a mecca for *Winter Sonata* fans around the world. Distinguished by its towering Dawn Redwoods and scenic walkways, the island is now essentially a *Winter Sonata* theme park, drawing large crowds on weekdays and weekends.

According to Gangwon Province officials, a record 330,000 foreign travelers visited the island in 2010 alone. Interestingly, Japanese tourists were significantly outnumbered by travelers from Thailand, Taiwan, China, and Malaysia—perhaps an indication of how the Korean drama boom has migrated across Asia.

Nami Island's increased status as a tourist attraction is also extending its life as a filming location. The Thai movie *Hello Stranger* (2010) was filmed on the island, as was the recent Malaysian soap opera *Calling of Nami Island*, which goes some way in explaining the sudden increase in tourist visits from this countries.

Hello Stranger

Jeju Island (*Jewel in the Palace, All In*)

Jeju Island has always been Korea's entry into the imaginary World's Greatest Places to Visit sweepstakes. So while it would be a stretch to say that the popularity of dramas like *Jewel in the Palace* and *All In* allowed Jeju to be "rediscovered," it certainly didn't hurt.

In *Jewel in the Palace*, Jeju is where lead character Janggeum ends up after being chased out of the palace in a conspiracy, and where she begins to train in Oriental medicine, which eventually enables her to fulfill her destiny as a royal physician. Naturally, many episodes of the drama were filmed at various locations around the island, including the Jeju Folk Museum, Odolgae, and Mt. Songak.

Jeju was also the main location for *All In*, and regional authorities have been eager to milk the drama's popularity to boost tourism. Much of the show was filmed at an indoor set near Seopjikoji, which was renamed the "*All In* House" and reopened to the public in June 2005. It has been described as the country's first "memorial hall" for any drama.

Yangju (*Jewel in the Palace*)

Much of the filming of *Jewel in the Palace* was done in an outdoor set in Yangju, Gyeonggi Province, which was designed as a Joseon era village. The 6,600 square meter site has since been rebuilt into the "Daejanggeum Theme Park," which continues to be a major tourist attraction.

Now an important part of Yangju Culture Valley, the park consists of 23 different rooms, including the Daejeon (king's residence), Daebijeon (queen's residence), Suragan (royal kitchen), Sojubang (kitchen for palace staff), and Gaeksa (guest house). Each room displays the costumes and props that were actually used by the actors and actresses during the filming of the drama.

Top K-Drama Stars

The Korean drama frenzy over the past decade has made some of the country's leading actors and actresses into household names in global living rooms. *Winter Sonata* stars Bae Yong-joon and Choi Ji-woo continue to be treated as royalty in Japan, while *Jewel in the Palace*'s Lee Young-ae is greeted with a rapturous welcome nearly every time she gets off a plane.

The three remain the biggest names in Hallyu, but younger heartthrobs like Jang Keun-suk and Hyun Bin appear to be knocking on the door of superstardom as well.

First-Generation K-Drama Stars

It was the Japanese success of *Winter Sonata*, *Jewel in the Palace, Autumn in My Heart*, and *Stairway to Heaven* that marked the beginning of an Asia-wide frenzy of Korean dramas in the 2000s. Naturally, the stars of the shows, including Bae Yong-joon, Choi Ji-woo, Lee Young-ae, Song Hye-kyo, Song Seung-hun, and Kwon Sang-woo, emerged as the early faces of Hallyu.

Bae Yong-joon

It remains to be seen whether any future Korean star will match the success of Bae Yong-joon, who is now counted among the global icons of the showbiz industry.

Born in Seoul in 1972, Bae emerged as one of the country's more popular celebrities after making his television debut in 1994. He was destined for greater things, however, and the immense success of *Winter Sonata* in Japan allowed him to shed his Clark Kent clothes and become "Yonsama."

Bae won a Best Actor award at the 2003 Blue Dragon Film Awards for his work in the film *Untold Scandal*, an adaptation of French novel *Les Liaisons Dangereuses* set in 18th century France. He returned to Korean television in 2008 with the fantasy action series *The Legend*, which landed him actor-of-the-year honors from MBC.

Bae was nominated by Korean tourism authorities as the goodwill ambassador for their "Visit Korea

Year" campaign from 2010 to 2012. He has also engaged in other activities to promote a younger and more fashionable image of the country.

As part of his efforts to promote Korea, Bae released a 2009 book titled *A Journey in Search of Korea's Beauty*, which was published in both Korean and English. The book includes essays and photos written and taken by Bae himself during his travels around Korea. With the help of eleven cultural experts—among them tea master Park Dong-chun, traditional costume designer Lee Hyo-jae, and traditional liquor maker Park Rok-dam—Bae managed to explore a wide range of cultural themes in food and beverages, attire, and artifacts.

Bae hasn't forgotten to reciprocate the love of his Japanese fans. He donated one billion won to a Japanese government organization to help the country's relief efforts following the earthquake and tsunami of March 2011.

Lee Young-ae

Lee Young-ae is the female star who comes closest to matching Bae's international influence. Born in 1971, Lee began her career as a fashion model in 1984 and made her acting debut in the early 1990s after gaining fame in television advertisements.

Her breakthrough moment came in 2000 when she earned critical acclaim as the female lead in *Joint Security Area*, the first film by director Park Chan-wook. Park went on to become one of Asia's definitive directors, with his 2003 film *Old Boy* winning the Grand Prix at the Cannes Film Festival the following year.

Lee was already one of the country's top-earning actresses when she was cast in the lead role in *Jewel in the Palace*. The rest, as they say, is history. The drama's borderless appeal earned Lee global fame.

Lee would go on to team up again with Park on the 2005 film *Sympathy for Lady Vengeance*. In what many consider as her best work as an actress, Lee plays Geum-ja, an ex-convict who tracks down a serial child murderer who ordered her to carry out a kidnapping, threatening to murder her newborn daughter if she refused. The role earned her Best Actress honors at the Blue Dragon Film Awards and the Paeksang Art Awards.

Lee's public image has benefited from her commitment to charity work throughout her career. She accompanied community workers on a trip to Ethiopia in 1997 and worked to assist poor children and orphans. Two years later, she flew to India to help members of the lowest caste. Named as a United Nations Children's Fund (UNICEF) goodwill ambassador in 2004, Lee has been involved in promoting various programs aimed at providing better access to education and improving healthcare facilities in poor countries. She has also made a number of personal donations to schools and hospitals around the world. One Chinese school she helped even renamed itself "Lee Young Ae Elementary School" as a gesture of appreciation.

Choi Ji-woo

Though she is now considered as one of the most celebrated actresses in Asia, *Winter Sonata* star Choi Ji-woo in fact had hard time breaking into the K-Entertainment industry at the beginning of her career.

Born in 1975, Choi won an audition to join KBS's acting stable in 1994. Her legacy as an artist will forever be her work co-starring with Bae Yong-joon in *Winter Sonata*, as the two have repeatedly crossed paths at critical moments in their careers.

Choi and Bae had never worked together before joining the cast of KBS's *First Love*, which aired its first episode in September 1996. This proved a breakthrough moment for both of them, as the show went on to become one of Korean television's all-time hits, scoring a 65.8 percent audience share for its final episode in April 1997, which remains the country's highest-ever viewership rating.

Choi was well received for her performance as a woman suffering from leukemia in the 2001 SBS drama *Beautiful Days*, which also featured another future Hallyu star, Lee Byung-hun.

Choi went on to display her magical onscreen chemistry with Bae again in *Winter Sonata* and extend her hot streak further with SBS's *Stairway to Heaven*, a romantic drama that also featured budding male star Kwon Sang-woo and was one of the most-watched shows of 2003. The immense success of *Winter Sonata* in Japan and other countries cemented Choi's reputation as one of the most bankable stars in Korean entertainment.

Since *Stairway to Heaven*, Choi has been taking more time off between projects. Her appearance on MBC's *Air City* in 2007 was her first in three years. In 2009, she starred opposite Yoo Ji-tae in the SBS drama *A Star's Lover*, playing a top actress who falls in love with an average Joe. She received 48 million won per episode, the highest salary for a Korean actress at the time.

Lee Byung-hun

Lee Byung-hun, born in 1970, emerged as a Hallyu star with his performance opposite actress Song Hye-kyo in the 2003 SBS hit drama *All In*. Lee has always been reliable in choosing the right projects. He singlehandedly converted his television fame into movie stardom with his first film, *Joint Security Area*, which also starred Lee Young-ae. The actor won critical acclaim for his role as a South Korean border patrol soldier who develops a risky friendship with a North Korean border guards. His performance would win him Best Actor honors at the Pusan Film Critics' Awards.

Lee went on to star with Choi Ji-woo in the 2001 hit SBS drama *Beautiful Days* before exploding into international stardom with *All In*, which had him cast as an enigmatic, troubled gambler. For his performance in the series, Lee received Best Actor honors at the Paeksang Arts Awards and the Actor of the Year title at SBS's year-end Drama Awards.

In 2005, Lee played a gangster, but not a small-time one or one that was down on his luck in *A Bittersweet Life*, a dark and gritty action thriller that premiered at the 2005 Cannes Film Festival. Lee's chemistry with *A Bittersweet Life* director Kim Ji-woon continued with the 2008 movie *The Good, the Bad, the Weird*.

Lee's surging acting career put him in demand for international projects. He co-starred with Hollywood star Josh Hartnett and Japanese megastar Takuya Kimura in the 2009 film *I Come With the Rain* and took the role the of the villainous Storm Shadow in *G.I. Joe: The Rise of Cobra*, which also featured Sienna Miller and Channing Tatum.

Lee then made a triumphant return to television with the KBS spy drama *Iris*, which also featured top Korean stars like Kim Tae-hee and Jung Jun-ho. The star-studded drama was shot in Hungary, Japan, and Korea and featured spectacular action sequences that seemed to have been inspired by American action-espionage series such as *24*.

Lee is also slated to return as Storm Shadow in the *G.I. Joe* sequel, which is being directed by Jon Chu and awaits release in the summer of 2012.

Song Hye-kyo

Born in 1981, Song Hye-kyo made her television debut in 1996 with a small role in *First Love*. She became a household name after appearing in the popular SBS sitcom *Soonpoong Clinic* in 1999. Her popularity rose to new heights the following year with *Autumn in My Heart*, which turned her into a transcendent star among Asian television viewers. Song continued her successful streak in television with *All In* and the 2004 KBS hit *Full House*.

Song was cast in the title role of the 2007 film *Hwang Jin-i*, based on a legendary 16th century *gisaeng* (a female artist who entertained aristocrats and kings). She made her US film debut the following year with *Fetish* before returning to Korean television for the 2008 KBS drama *The World That They Live In*.

In the recent film *Today*, Song Hye-kyo plays Da-hye, a documentary producer who forgives the 15-year-old boy who killed her fiancé. Critics and audiences alike remarked on the depth of her performance, with its rich expression of the character's turmoil and grief.

Song Seung-hun

Born in 1976, Song Seung-hun began his career as a fashion model in 1995. He would go on to become a household name after appearing in the MBC sitcom *Three Guys and Three Girls* in 1996.

His popularity peaked in 2000 after he starred opposite Song Hye-kyo in the KBS romantic drama *Autumn in My Heart*, the first installment of the four-part *Endless Love* drama series by director Yoon Seok-ho. *Autumn in My Heart* scored huge ratings in Korea and was well received by viewers in several Asian countries, boosting the popularity of Song and his co-stars, including Won Bin.

In 2002, Song was cast in the action-comedy film *Make It Big* and co-starred with popular Asian actresses Karen Mok, Shu Qi, and Zhao Wei in the Hong Kong film *So Close*. Song returned to television with Yoon Seok-ho's *Summer Scent* in 2003. He also performed in such films as *Ice Rain* and *He Was Cool*. Song would go on to star opposite Lee Yeon-hee in the 2008 hit MBC drama *East of Eden* and appear in the 2010 Korean remake of *A Better Tomorrow*, the iconic 1986 Hong Kong action film starring Chow Yun-fat and Leslie Cheung. Song reunited with Kim Tae-hee for the 2011 MBC romantic comedy *My Princess*, which managed above-average viewership ratings in Korea.

Kwon Sang-woo

Born in 1976, Kwon Sang-woo started out as a fashion model in the 1990s. His rare combination of boyish face and Greek god physique soon began to land him small parts in movies and television shows.

He starred opposite Kim Ha-neul in the 2003 romantic comedy *My Tutor Friend*, which was a surprise box office hit that solidified Kwon's status as one of the country's most popular young actors. His popularity hit a new peak with *Stairway to Heaven*, which scored huge ratings in Korea and was eventually exported across Asia and to the Middle East and Central and South American countries like Mexico, Peru, and Chile. Many consider Kwon's performance as a troubled high school student in the 2004 film *Once Upon a Time in High School* to represent the definitive work of his career so far. The movie was a massive box office hit and drew raves from critics for its disturbing depiction of school life under the authoritarian society of the 1970s.

Kwon has attempted to use his *Stairway to Heaven* fame to reach an international audience. He has signed on to co-star in an upcoming film with Hong Kong superstars Jackie Chan and Cecilia Cheung.

Next Generation K-Drama Stars

The likes of Bae Yong-joon, Lee Young-ae, Choi Ji-woo, and Lee Byung-hun certainly set the bar high for the next generation of Korean entertainers.

But the serious buzz generated by a number of young stars like Song Hye-kyo, Hyun Bin, and Jang Keun-suk suggests they are prepared to be handed the torch.

Hyun Bin

Born in 1982, Hyun Bin became a household name starring opposite Kim Sun-ah in the 2005 MBC hit *My Lovely Samsoon*, a romantic comedy. The drama was one of the most widely watched television shows of the year.

Hyun attempted to extend his success to movies, appearing with Chinese star Tang Wei in the 2010 film *Late Autumn*.

Hyun's popularity reached new levels after his appearance in the SBS romantic comedy *Secret Garden*, which co-starred actress Ha Ji-won. *Secret Garden* was Korea's most watched show for the first half of 2011, and Hyun, who played a young department store owner falling in love with a movie stuntwoman, found himself buried under a massive pile of endorsement deals as advertisers clamored for his services.

Hyun went on to appear in the 2011 film *Come Rain, Come Shine*, which was featured at the Berlin International Film Festival. In 2011, Hyun Bin drew the attention of appreciation from the Korean public when he put his raging popularity behind him and joined the Marines for a 21-month stint of mandatory military service.

Jang Keun-suk

Born in 1987, Jang Keun-suk has, like Bae Yong-joon, enjoyed immense popularity with his work in Japan. He appeared in the 2003 MBC sitcom *Nonstop 4*, drawing attention as an up-and-coming young celebrity. His breakthrough moment came in 2008, when he was cast in the hit MBC drama *Beethoven Virus*, one of the most widely watched shows of the year. Jang drew critical acclaim for his performance in the 2009 film *The Case of Itaewon Homicide*, a thriller inspired by a real-life murder case that took place in 1997 at a hamburger restaurant in Seoul's Itaewon neighborhood. Jang played the role of Pearson, a disturbed young Korean-American accused of stabbing a student to death.

In *You're Beautiful*, Jang played Hwang Tae-kyung, the leader of rock band A.N.Jell, who falls in love with a female band member masquerading as a man. The drama became a phenomenal hit in Korea and Japan as well as other Asian countries. Jang played another musician in *Mary Stayed Out All Night*, this time the leader of an indie rock band who finds himself entangled in a fake marriage.

Alone in Love appealed to many viewers with its realistic approach to a love story.

The Slave Hunters opened up new horizons for the period drama.

© KBS

Mary Stayed Out All Night was hugely popular in Japan and Taiwan in 2011.

Jang Keun-suk Fever in Japan

Will Korea ever produce another Bae Yong-joon? While the jury still appears to be out on the question given the impressive depth, breadth, and longevity of Bae's influence, the imminent superstardom of Jang Keun-suk is beginning to push the needle toward "yes." Since the huge Japanese success of the SBS drama *You're Beautiful* in 2010, Jang's popularity has been reaching a fever pitch reminiscent of the days when Yonsama took Japan by storm.

The outbreak of Jang fever had *the Asahi Shimbun*, one of Japan's leading media outlets, feeling it needed to write something about it.

"The frenzy over the actor, who is tall and lean with effeminate looks—just like a character in a comic book for teenage girls—

shows no sign of abating," the newspaper wrote in its edition of July 24, 2011. The article went on to describe how Jang's presence was becoming ubiquitous in television commercials and print advertisements, and how a certain Korean liquor brand sold more than 350,000 cases in just two months in Japan after the Korean star began representing it. "The trajectory of Jang's popularity seems to parallel that of Bae," the newspaper observed. "Experts say Jang's swift ascent to stardom in Japan shows that Japanese women are not just looking for men with handsome faces and bodybuilder bodies."

The Asahi Shimbun's weekly publication *Aera* dedicated a five-page feature to analyzing Jang's rising popularity in Japan. The article went so far as to suggest what would have been considered blasphemy just months earlier—that Jang's star was now threatening to outshine Yonsama's.

It seems that Jang shares many attributes with Bae, although he isn't the same entertainer. Like Bae, Jang combines a quiet intensity with gentle charisma. Like Bae, Jang is a noted perfectionist notorious for his work ethic in preparing for roles. Both Korean stars go out of their way to show they care about their fans. Perhaps the biggest difference between Jang and Bae is the ages of the fans screaming their names. Bae is considered a divine presence by many Japanese middle-aged women, whereas Jang's fans are spread more over different generations, ranging from teenagers to senior citizens.

Jang's debut single "Let Me Cry" soared to No. 1 on Japan's Oricon Chart in the first week of his album's release in April 2011, selling 119,000 copies. This made him the first non-Japanese male solo artist in 30 years to top the chart in his opening week.

Korean Pop Stars Bring New Blood to Dramas

With television dramas burgeoning into a global business, more and more Korean pop stars are rushing to film sets to prove they have a little acting in them, too. And studios are greeting them with open arms as they look to exploit the rising popularity of K-pop to promote their new dramas.

The blueprint was laid out by Rain, the Hallyu megastar who has managed to balance successful careers in both acting and music. After gaining fame as a singer, Rain made his acting debut with the 2003 KBS series *Sang Doo! Let's Go to School*, which landed him Best New Actor honors at KBS's year-end drama awards. He reached a new peak in his acting career starring opposite Song Hye-kyo in *Full House*, which won him more fans across Asia. Rain played the lead in the 2010 KBS action-adventure series *The Fugitive: Plan B*, heading an all-star cast that also featured Lee Na-young, Daniel Henney, and Japanese actors Uehara Takako and Naoto Takanaka.

A newer role model for success is Kim Hyun-joong, a member of popular boy band SS501 who found international fame with his performance in the 2009 KBS megahit *Boys Over Flowers*, one of the many television adaptations of the iconic Japanese manga series of the same name. Kim appeared the following year in MBC's *Naughty Kiss*, the latest Korean drama to be exported across different time zones.

Park Yu-chun, leader of the boy band JYJ and a former member of the immensely popular TVXQ, is among the most active singers-turned-actors. He was well received for his role in the 2010 KBS hit *Sungkyunkwan Scandal*, a teen romance set in 18th century Korea; the performance would get him named Best New Actor at the broadcaster's year-end drama awards. Park recently starred with veteran drama stars Lee Da-hae and Kim Seung-woo in the 2011 MBC drama *Miss Ripley*, which drew mixed reviews from viewers and critics.

Jung Yong-hwa, a singer with the rock group CN Blue, recently followed up his supporting role in *You're Beautiful* by portraying a guitar-playing art school student in the 2011 MBC romantic drama *Heartstrings*.

No drama has relied more on pop music talent than the recent KBS series *Dream High*, the product of a collaboration between Bae Yong-joon's Key East and music industry giant JYP Entertainment. The cast of *Dream High* reads like a who's who of the country's top young pop stars. Taecyeon and Wooyeon from boy band 2PM; Suzy and Enjung from girl bands Miss A and T-ara, respectively; and female solo artist IU appeared in this story of the lives and loves of high school students who share the dream of becoming musicians. The drama managed above-average ratings and was renewed for a second season, which is scheduled to hit the airwaves in January 2012.

From Little Acorns . . .

Europe and the US launched their first television networks in the 1930s, Japan in 1953. Korea, in contrast, was something of a late starter. It took until 1956 for the country to get its first TV network, and even longer— until the early 1960s—for that network to reach any real level of activity. Furthermore, the dramas back then were fraught with problems across the production process—a symptom of the times. Most of these were resolved by 1987, around the time a democracy was setting firm roots in the country. These improvements go some way in explaining the marked difference in quality between Korean films and dramas before and after the 1980s. The change was quite dramatic, calling to mind the way Koreans succeeded in picking up the pieces after the Korean War and modernizing their country seemingly overnight. The dramas of the 1980s show the country's established values clashing with those of a new era.

The 1990s saw the emergence of dramas that built on this foundation by blending traditional values from the past with the currents of a new era, adding in more universal elements and newer, freer ideas developed by creators who had grown up watching American and Japanese TV series in their formative years.

This mixture of nostalgia for older values, fresh ideas from a new era, and subject matter from a variety of cultural influences proved equally appealing to overseas viewers. The Korean dramas that global audiences enjoy today have storylines about affection (with a focus on the traditional family), the purest of love, and success stories in which characters achieve human victories.

The lead performers in these dramas have also been essential to their success. From Bae Yong-joon and Lee Young-ae in the earlier days of the boom to Jang Keun-suk more recently, the stars in Korean dramas appeal to overseas fans with their idiosyncrasies and charm. They have also maintained their popularity by keeping in constant touch with their overseas fan bases—appearing on local networks and showing up at fan meetings.

The changes continue. Historical dramas now deal with a wider range of subject matter, focusing not just on the royal court but on commoners and slaves, too. There is a constant striving to develop something new: more diverse and universal stories, bold and polished Hollywood-style productions. *The Slave Hunters* and *Iris* exemplify this trend.

The drama is arguably the most everyday example of popular culture, reflecting the issues, daily life, and sensibilities of a particular society at a particular time. To move viewers, it needs both an eye-catching visual style and universal themes that resonate with a wide audience.

If the makers of Korean drama can grasp its strengths, preserve its universal appeal to the countries of the world, incorporate the polish of foreign productions, and work with other countries in cultural exchange, they can lay to rest any fears of a "Korean drama bubble" and develop a soft power that goes beyond mere popularity. And they can succeed in presenting an attractive cultural product for the world to share in as a whole.

Further Reading

Books on K-Drama

Chua, B. H., & Iwabuchi, K. (Eds) (2008) *East Asian Pop Culture: Analysing the Korean Wave*. Hong Kong: Hong Kong University Press

Jung, S. (2011) *Korean Masculinities and Transcultural Consumption: Yonsama, Rain, Oldboy, K-Pop Idols*. Hong Kong: Hong Kong University Press

Kim, D. K., Kim, M. S. (Eds) (2011) *Hallyu: Influence of Korean Popular Culture in Asia and Beyond*. Seoul: Seoul National University Press

Kim, T. (2011) *Korean Wave: Global Popularity of Korean Drama*: Kindle Edition

Leto, J. (2011) *Asian Invasion! The Korean Wave of Popular Culture Washes Upon Many Shores: K-dramas*. Webster's Digital Services

Nichols, R. (2011) *Modern Korean Drama: An Anthology*. New York: Columbia University Press

Russell, M. J. (2008) *Pop Goes Korea: Behind the Revolution in Movies, Music, and Internet Culture*. Berkeley: Stone Bridge Press

Korea's "Big three" Networks

KBS	www.kbs.co.kr
MBC	www.imbc.com
SBS	www.sbs.co.kr

Websites on K-Drama

www.hulu.com

www.soompi.com

www.dramafever.com

www.dramabeans.com

www.koreandrama.org

www.dramacrazy.net

www.hancinema.net

www.koreanfilm.org

www.koreanmovie.com

www.korean-drama-guide.com

Organizations

Korea Foundation for International Culture Exchange   www.kofice.co.kr
Korea Tourist Organization   www.visitkorea.or.kr
Korea Creative Content Agency   www.kocca.kr

CREDITS

Planner   Wi Tack-Whan
Writer   Chung Ah-young
Copy Editor   Colin Mouat

Edited & Designed by Seoul Selection

Photographs